W9-DCZ-781

Why Things Go Wrong

BOOKS BY LAURENCE J. PETER

WHY THINGS GO WRONG
PETER'S ALMANAC
PETER'S PEOPLE
PETER'S QUOTATIONS
THE PETER PLAN
INDIVIDUAL INSTRUCTION
CLASSROOM INSTRUCTION
THERAPEUTIC INSTRUCTION
TEACHER EDUCATION
THE PETER PRESCRIPTION
THE PETER PRINCIPLE *(WITH RAYMOND HULL)*
PRESCRIPTIVE TEACHING

Why Things Go Wrong

——— OR ———

The Peter Principle Revisited

Dr. Laurence J. Peter

WILLIAM MORROW AND COMPANY, INC.
New York

HD
38
P449
1984

Copyright © 1985 by Laurence J. Peter

Illustrations from *Punch* reproduced by permission.
Drawings on pages 25, 37, 42, and 49 copyright Punch/Rothco.

All rights reserved. No part of this book may be reproduced or utilized in any
form or by any means, electronic or mechanical, including photocopying, recording or by any information storage and retrieval system, without permission in
writing from the Publisher. Inquiries should be addressed to Permissions Department, William Morrow and Company, Inc., 105 Madison Ave., New York, N.Y.
10016.

Library of Congress Cataloging in Publication Data

Peter, Laurence J.
    Why things go wrong, or, The Peter principle
revisited.

    1. Management—Anecdotes, facetiae, satire, etc.
I. Title. II. Title: Peter principle revisited.
HD38.P449 1984   658'.002'07   84-1192
ISBN 0-688-03902-2

Printed in the United States of America

First Edition

1 2 3 4 5 6 7 8 9 10

BOOK DESIGN BY BERNARD SCHLEIFER

101673

To STEPHEN PILE, *who believes that success is overrated, and whose glorification of failure everywhere should be a consolation to each of us as we confront our own areas of incompetence*

Contents

Why Things Go Wrong

1

A Man of Principle

The Peter Principle: In a hierarchy individuals tend to rise to their levels of incompetence. —LAURENCE J. PETER

I am plagued with doubt—I am not quite sure whether the world is run by incompetents who are sincere or by wise guys who are putting us on. Consider the following evidence and you will understand my dilemma. When I was a professor at the University of British Columbia, I received a memo that stated, "Professors who have no secretaries of their own may take advantage of the girls in the secretarial pool." The Stoughton, Wisconsin, *Courier* reported: "The Forton Street bridge was repaired following its collapse last fall. New iron end plates that held the truss were installed and the bridge is now in the same condition it was prior to its collapse." A help-wanted column carried this ad: "Person to work on nuclear fissionable isotope molecular reactive counters and three phase cyclotronic uranium photosynthesizers. No experience necessary." The *San Francisco Examiner* carried this news item: *"East Greenwich, R.I.* State transportation officials say there was no excuse for a maintenance crew that painted a yellow traffic stripe over a dead dog lying alongside a highway."

In my search for truth, I have persisted in my efforts to understand the underlying reasons for so many things going wrong, even though I am seldom certain whether an apparent manifes-

tation of incompetence is the sincere striving of a dedicated dolt
or the hoax of a bluffing buffoon.

The search for truth is really a lot of good fun.
—VERNON HOWARD

QUIT WHILE YOU ARE BEHIND

I began my last full-time employment in an established hierarchy in 1966, when I became a professor of education at the
University of Southern California. This position provided me with
endless opportunities to rise above my level of competence and
become a victim of my own principle. During my preceding
twenty-eight years in education I had progressed from student-
teacher to classroom teacher, to department head, to counselor,
to psychologist, to administrator of mental health services, to
university professor. In each position I had felt creative, confident, and competent, but at this final level I felt fulfilled. The
teaching was rewarding. My research projects challenged my
creative abilities, and the outcome of my studies gave me a sense
of achievement. The operation of my center for handicapped
children provided great satisfaction and a continuing learning
experience for me. I thought I had reached my level of optimal
effectiveness in my chosen profession, where I was regularly
experiencing the joy of accomplishment that comes from working on projects of intense personal interest.

Do what you can, with what you have, where you
are.   —THEODORE ROOSEVELT

My immediate superior was transferred and I was offered a
promotion to department head. Feeling that my present position
was the actualization of a long-held dream, I declined. Others
urged me not to be so hasty, to think it over. During the next
weeks I was encouraged from above and pressured from all sides
to accept the promotion. The stress thus created caused me dis-
comfort, so I decided to employ creative incompetence. This is

the technique of being deliberately incompetent in something completely irrelevant to your area of accomplishment. The purpose is to convince your superior that although you are competent in your present position you are unworthy of promotion. It may sound difficult, but in practice I found it quite easy and a lot of fun. Once a week I parked my car in the dean's parking space and the offers of promotion stopped.

Unfortunately, I received a Phi Delta Kappa research award which resulted in renewed efforts to promote me. Once more, creative incompetence came to the rescue. When the dean dropped by to consult me on a technical matter, I reached into a desk drawer and took out a dart, which I aimed at a target hanging on my office wall. I wrote down the number I had impaled, made a rapid calculation, and then gave him the answer to his question. He never seemed to catch on that I had known the answer all along. This did not surprise me, because I had noticed that generally, if you told the dean a joke, you had to say it was a joke or he wouldn't know he was supposed to laugh. This dean was so humorless that even the other deans noticed it.

I knew the dart strategy was a success when I overheard him say, "Peter is a genius, but he's a ding-a-ling." Once again the attempts to promote me ceased. The role of department head had been assigned temporarily to a professor who was only a few months from retirement. With the specter of a topless department fast approaching, endeavors to promote me were renewed yet again. At one memorable staff meeting I was aware that something was up when everyone treated me with excessive politeness and profuse flattery. The chairman called the meeting to order and announced the first item of business: the selection of a new department chairman. Each professor then promised me complete loyalty and cooperation if I would accept the promotion. They volunteered to write the grant proposals, to do the budget and all the hard work. All I would have to do would be to sit in my office, sign some papers, and take all the glory. Although the picture they painted was seductive and I did not doubt their good intentions, I was struck by the contrast between their promises and their usual infighting, backbiting, and petty paranoia. I was reminded of the old saying "Professors are so aggressive because the stakes are so small."

How could I turn down the utopia they painted? How could I reject their proffered love, loyalty, appreciation, and cooperation? The situation called for desperate measures. In silence I looked around the room and into the pleading eyes of each of my co-workers. I gazed at the ceiling as if expecting the answer to come from Above. I got up slowly and walked to the window, took out a cigarette and then a magnifying glass. I focused the sun's rays on the end of the cigarette and patiently waited until the tobacco ignited. Placing the cigarette between my lips, I took a puff and slowly exhaled a thin stream of smoke. All eyes were on me as I walked calmly back to my seat. Complete silence had descended upon the meeting. After a lengthy pause the chairman looked at his notes, cleared his throat, and said, "I think we had better go on to the next item on the agenda." Creative incompetence had triumphed once again.

Through the judicious practice of creative incompetence and the application of the power of negative thinking, I was able to stay at my level of competence until the success of the book *The Peter Principle* made it possible for me to escape from the university and continue my research independent of any hierarchical organization. The story of my adventure on the way to this happy state and my recollections of the main events leading to the discovery of the Peter Principle follow.

A QUEST FOR COMPETENCE

The first phase of my pursuit of competence began in 1938, when I took my first teacher education course, and continued until 1963—a period in which I took professional or higher-education courses each year. Did those twenty-five years of study mean I was the ultimate incompetent scholar or simply that I had been confused for longer than anyone else? I'll never know,

"What is it that teachers do that causes children to learn?"

but my explanation for my persistent search for knowledge is that early in my career I became intrigued with the question "What is it that teachers do that causes children to learn?"

This question entered my consciousness during a World War II teacher shortage. I had taken education courses and had obtained a credential that designated me a qualified teacher. I assumed this meant I had acquired special knowledge and skills not possessed by nonmembers of the profession.

> I prefer the company of peasants because they have
> not been educated sufficiently to reason incorrectly.
> —Montaigne

Because of the shortage of certificated high school teachers, temporary teaching permits were granted to persons qualified in a particular subject but lacking specific teacher education. Ben E. Fitz,* a co-worker in my department, was teaching on a tem-

*Names of some persons have been changed to protect the innocent and the guilty.

porary (war emergency) permit. When I became aware that his teaching was much like mine and that student achievement was similar in both our classes, I was somewhat disconcerted. What had I learned in all those teacher-education classes? Why was I not a better teacher than Ben, who had not set foot in a teacher-education institution? Had I been fooling myself into believing education courses were important and relevant to the teaching function? These questions sparked my interest in teacher competence and how it is acquired.

> Successful teachers are effective in spite of the psychological theories they suffer under.
>
> —Educational proverb

A Supercompetent

In 1943, I taught in a basement room in Central Elementary School in Chilliwack, British Columbia, Canada. In the other basement room, Mrs. Abel taught first grade. My first impression of Mrs. Abel was of a short, plump, middle-aged woman with gray hair combed up into a large neat bun on top of her head. She wore black walking shoes and was dressed, as always, in a navy-blue skirt and white blouse. Her most impressive characteristics were her manner and speech. She had an aura of complete calm and she looked directly at whomever she spoke to. I had been warned by the principal that the other teachers found her impossible to get along with but that she was a wonderful teacher and the children and their parents loved and admired her. Later, he told me of a problem he had: All the parents of first-graders wanted their children to be in Mrs. Abel's class because she was known throughout the district as the best teacher of beginning reading and writing.

It was not long before I understood why she did not get along with the school staff. She attended only the first staff meeting of the school year and did not go to in-service meetings or school social functions. She preferred to eat her lunch in her classroom with her pupils rather than in the staff lunchroom. She told me she was the best first-grade teacher in the district and the other teachers didn't know what they were doing. When they sought her help or advice, she replied, "I have developed techniques that work for me. Why don't you develop techniques that work for you?" Asked how her pupils all learned to read in the first few weeks of school, when other teachers took all year to achieve the same results, she answered, "Because my techniques are superior to theirs."

> A teacher affects eternity; no one can tell where his
> influence stops.   —HENRY ADAMS

When the principal realized that my interest in Mrs. Abel was motivated not by idle curiosity about her idiosyncratic behavior, but by my admiration for her ability, he shared some background information with me. She had graduated from the local high school forty-four years earlier and had attended the Provincial Normal School for one year of teacher training. She returned home to Chilliwack and became a first-grade teacher. Except for three years—during which she was married, had a daughter, and became a widow—she had remained a first-grade teacher. In spite of the promptings of the superintendent and others, she steadfastly refused to upgrade her qualifications or to take in-service courses. When pressed, she said, "Do they know any more than I about teaching?" When urged to get a degree so she would be eligible for promotion, she replied, "I don't want a promotion. I don't want to be an administrator. I like working with children, not adults."

> Why in the world are salaries higher for administra-
> tors when the basic mission is teaching?
>   —GOVERNOR JERRY BROWN

I can only speculate on why Mrs. Abel invited me into her classroom and shared her ideas with me, but my first visit convinced me I was in the presence of genius. Although my observations, over a two-year period, were merely glimpses of a brilliantly conceived and effectively implemented teaching program, I offer here some of my perceptions along with Mrs. Abel's explanations of her methods.

The First Day. In the 1940's there were no kindergarten or preschool programs in this rural area, so Mrs. Abel began by introducing her pupils to school routines. After the children were settled and eager for their first lesson, she hung a chart at the front of the room picturing three red apples. She said, "We are going to learn a rhyme about these apples." She chanted slowly: "How many apples do you see? You can count them, one, two, three." She then had the class recite the poem in unison, following the beat she marked with her hand. When she was certain that all the children were participating, she turned over the picture, revealing:

She pointed to the words and beat time as before while the children chanted the words. As the final activity of the day, she passed out mimeographed copies of the rhyme and the children recited it as they pointed to the words. It was a happy group of children who left school that first day, and I expect that families throughout the district were surprised when their one-day scholars pointed to the words and "read" the apple poem.

> The mediocre teacher tells. The good teacher explains. The superior teacher demonstrates. The great teacher inspires.   —WILLIAM ARTHUR WARD

Mrs. Abel explained: "I start with words and objects with which the children are familiar. Children accomplish the most complex learning achievement of their lives—to speak their native tongue—without formal instruction. The sound of the word *apple* is a symbol that in no way resembles an apple. Neither does the visual representation of the word: APPLE. If the child can speak the word, reading the word should present no problems. Therefore I teach the children to say the words, and then show them the words."

I was in no position to question her theory, but I was certainly impressed with the results she achieved. Systematically she progressed to longer rhymes and then used the words from them in other contexts. The children read from the first day and progressed rapidly. Their joy of accomplishment was obvious. When they used the prescribed readers, they completed them in less than half the usual time and were able to engage in substantial supplemental reading.

In every detail of teaching, Mrs. Abel seemed to have a system that worked. Her program was developmentally sequenced to assure that every child acquired each component skill required for reading, writing, and elementary arithmetic. Her ability to observe each child, so that no essential accomplishment was missed, was phenomenal. In answer to my questions, she gave precise and lucid explanations:

"There is an old saying, 'The eye of the farmer fattens the flock.' I can believe that. Much of my success is because I detect when any child is having difficulty. That's why no child in my class gets left behind. Once a child is left behind, the problems of cumulative error can result in development of a learning disability. The eye of the teacher strengthens the child's learning."

And another: "The reading experts are divided into two camps. One group promotes phonics as the royal road to learning, and the other believes that the look-and-say method will produce more happy little readers. Can you believe that intelligent adults would waste their time on such a silly argument? Good teaching includes both methods, but not as separate approaches. Take the word *can* in the apple rhyme. The children see the word and say the word. Then we play a game on one of my charts, changing only the last letter, starting with *can* and going on to *cat, cab, car, cap.* Then we start with *can* and change only the first letter: *an, fan, man, tan, pan, van.* After they have worked with all the vowels and consonants in this way, they can read phonetically many one-syllable words. Then we combine some of these words and they read *hatbox, dustpan, dishpan, tomcat, fishpond, handbag, bathtub, lipstick,* and so forth. I just keep increasing their sight vocabulary, their word-analysis skills, and phonics by building on their experience and the poems and stories we read. These techniques are an integrated process in my teaching and are not competitive techniques, as the experts like to believe."

She told me that years ago the superintendent had encouraged her to take courses in psychology. She said, "When I asked why, he told me it might help me to understand the children better. I told him that as a teacher I was more concerned that the children understand me."

For a number of years she had resolutely declined invitations to demonstrate her methods for other teachers, but in her last year before retirement she weakened. She and I shared a store-room. A few days before the teachers' convention I discovered that she had moved some teaching material out of storage and had replaced it with material she used in the classroom. When I asked her why, she said, "I'm storing the things that work best for me and showing them the stuff that I no longer use. It's taken me forty years to develop my technique and they're not getting it for nothing."

Educational authorities would give Mrs. Abel very low marks for attitude, cooperation with co-workers, in-service education, professional advancement, use of new audiovisual materials, and application of approved teaching methods. I wish that she had shared her teaching techniques more freely, that she had been more open to new ideas, and that she had improved her own educational background. The fact remains, in spite of her idio-syncrasies and lack of "professionalism," she was one of that select group of superteachers. Her students had great enthusiasm for school and read better and learned more than any other first-graders I have encountered.

> Teaching is not a lost art, but regard for it is a lost
> tradition.   —JACQUES BARZUN

Probably the key to Mrs. Abel's success was her sensitivity to feedback. She was acutely aware of her students' responses to her instruction. The children's learning told her which of her methods were effective. Her experience showed her which things to reject and which to retain for future lessons. Her sensitivity to her own effectiveness shaped her teaching performance. Each teaching experience was a learning experience for her, so that she grew in competence throughout her whole career.

> Most educators would continue to lecture on navi-
> gation while the ship is going down.
>   —JAMES H. BOREN

More Competents

During the next ten years I met many outstanding teachers—including Mr. Julius, who had developed a system of simulation games that taught retarded children practical self-care, traffic safety, housekeeping, and other socially valuable skills. He enriched the life of every child in his classes at the provincial residential school for retarded children. I admired the work of Mr. Query, who taught gifted high school students. He stimulated their superior mental abilities by his powerful challenges and his tenacious questioning. Ann Cestery taught social studies by having her students research their own homes and community. They did so well they were given awards by the British Columbia Historical Society and the British Columbia Research Council. I studied what these and other highly successful teachers did to achieve their outstanding results. In almost every case their effectiveness was the result of original or unorthodox methods, and not those acquired in teacher education.

Years later, I was not surprised when I read the results of a research project conducted by Dr. James Popham of UCLA in which he studied teacher effectiveness.* More than two thousand students were instructed by fully qualified, certificated teachers, and by persons educated in relevant subject matter who had not taken any courses in teacher education. He called the former group *teachers,* and the latter, *nonteachers.* There was no statistically significant difference, in the amount the students learned, between teachers and nonteachers.

A Year in Jail

In 1947, I became an instructor in the British Columbia prison system, working with male inmates seventeen to twenty-three years of age. Up to this time, teaching had been a pleasant and

*W. J. Popham, "Performance Tests of Teaching Proficiency: Rationale, Development, and Validation," *American Educational Research Journal* (January 1971).

satisfying job which repeatedly brought me the joy of accomplishment. Teaching prisoners was a humbling experience. Some of my brighter students found the prison recreational activities boring, so to provide a challenge I introduced them to chess. I first taught the names of the pieces and the basic moves. After a few minutes play, I noticed Tony had lost his queen to his opponent's pawn. Tony asked me, "What the hell do I do now? He just took my bitch with his pimp." Ten minutes into the game Tony had destroyed my lesson on the names used in chess.

My counseling did not fare much better. Mario told me the story of the events that led to his imprisonment. Each adventure he described was clear evidence of his incompetence as a criminal. While stealing a truckload of produce from a warehouse, he had become panicky and had stopped for a smoke. Nervously removing his cigarettes from his pocket, he failed to notice he had dropped his driver's license on the floor. A burglar who leaves his name and address at the scene of the crime is hardly a challenge to law enforcement officers. He stole a 1,500-pound spool of new trolley cable. Because the hydro company owned all the trolley wire in the province, it was obvious, when he attempted to sell it as scrap metal, that he possessed stolen property. He was arrested. In a breaking-and-entering attempt, after picking the lock he found his entry still barred by a safety chain. He decided he needed a hacksaw, but set off the burglar alarm while breaking into a hardware store to obtain one.

When he finished the recital of his criminal misadventures, he said, "Mr. Peter, as I look back over my mistakes I realize why I am in trouble." This was the moment of truth that gladdens a counselor's heart: the counselee's insight into his problem. "Mario," I said, "you have made a big step forward. You now realize where you went wrong." He raised his head, his eyes met mine, and slowly and deliberately he said, "Yes! My mistake was I hired a bum lawyer."

On a test I asked: "_____ is the best policy." Every inmate filled the blank with the right answer: *honesty*.

After a year at the prison, I returned to the public school

system. I had learned there is a big gap between what people know and what they do.

My prison experience influenced my future career in two ways. First, I observed a common characteristic among my students: a lack of impulse control. Their ability to delay gratification appeared to be retarded. I determined that in my teaching I would do what was within my power to encourage appropriate levels of impulse control. Second, I enrolled in anthropology, sociology, and criminology courses in an attempt to acquire a better understanding of the influence of society and culture on normal and criminal human behavior.

A Lucky Break

In 1953, I was awarded a fellowship sponsored jointly by the Canadian Mental Health Association, the Federal Department of Health, and the Provincial Department of Education for an interdisciplinary study of mental health practices and services. On completion of this program I served as the coordinator of mental health services for a community of schools. During my ten years on that job I made thousands of observations of teachers in action in their classrooms. It was the perfect opportunity to continue my search for answers to my questions about teacher competence. I developed a system for identifying and recording specific incidences of teachers' effectively promoting student learning.

The Subject Was Not All Roses

Although my search was for competence, it was inevitable that I would also observe some incompetence. Ty Rade, an elementary principal, was upset by the noise in classrooms during the short break between periods when teachers changed classrooms. He hurried to his office and announced over the P.A. system: "From now on, no teacher shall leave a classroom until

She got a job as a classroom teacher and reached her level of incompetence after an incredibly short trip.

His students hung on his every word.

the other teacher arrives.'' Bea Gin, a reading specialist, had so many reading-readiness activities for her students that they spent most of their time telling stories, looking at pictures, and engaging in a variety of visual perception exercises, and the year was up before she got to the reading lessons. Alma Mater, a high school librarian, had a preoccupation with the orderly arrangement of books on the library shelves, so she expended much of her energies in trying to keep students from using the books.

At first I thought of these examples as a waste product of my research, but later came to see them as a useful by-product. When called upon to talk about my study of teacher competence, I used some of the amusing examples of incompetence as comic relief in my serious presentations.

My first example was a teacher I called Miss Ditto because she had about as much creativity as a duplicating machine. In teacher's college she had been the perfect student. She was punctual, obedient, and wrote down everything the professor said.

Her class notes looked like a carbon copy of the professor's lecture notes. She was such a good student she had no problem taking courses and somehow survived practice teaching. She got a job as a classroom teacher and reached her level of incompetence after an incredibly short trip. Although she was a competent consumer of knowledge, she was a flop as a dispenser of it. Her broad educational background meant only that she could be boring in any subject in the curriculum. She was the kind of person who could light up a room simply by leaving it. If it weren't for her red hair she would have been completely colorless. She won't get fired because she is punctual, obedient, and fills in all the forms on time. The only thing she can't do is teach. So she will remain a teacher for the rest of her career, boring the children, frustrating the parents, and driving the principal out of his mind.

The principal of the school, Mr. Blunt, had the most straightforward way of missing the point of anyone I ever met. He had been a competent scholar and an excellent teacher. His students hung on his every word and he never experienced discipline problems. When he became principal, he had little understanding or sympathy for the average teacher and his or her concerns. He was confused by the discovery that although he got on so well with children, he had nothing but trouble in relating to his staff and the officials in the superintendent's office. He is not eligible for further promotion and spends much of his time reminiscing about the good old days back in the classroom. A competent teacher of children promoted to be an incompetent manager of adults.

The superintendent of schools, Dr. Pennywise, tried to economize on items like chalk, paper, and crayons while wasting large sums on unproven electronic gadgetry. Throughout his teaching career, and while he was a school principal, his wife had taken his paycheck and given him a weekly allowance, but as superintendent he was in charge of a multimillion-dollar operation. A competent teacher promoted to be an incompetent financial administrator.

A PRINCIPLE IS NAMED

In my lectures I called this phenomenon THE PETER PRIN-CIPLE: In a hierarchy individuals tend to rise to their levels of incompetence.

I named it a principle because it described a generalization or a tendency and not something inevitable. There are competent teachers like Mrs. Abel who declined to join the race to the top. Even with her problems in relating to adults, she had been encouraged to take courses and obtain a degree so she would be eligible for promotion. As an educator of teachers or as an administrator she surely would have been a victim of the Peter Principle. The system encourages individuals to climb to their levels of incompetence. If you are able to do your job efficiently and with ease, you will be told your job lacks challenge and you should move up. The problem is that when you find something you can't do very well, that is where you stay, bungling the job, frustrating your co-workers, and eroding the effectiveness of the organization.

The Unexpected

When I gave public lectures on my teacher-competence research and used the Peter Principle to add humor and to make some points about incompetence, I talked only about education and my study. To my surprise, after the question period people would share such confidences as: "You must know about our company! I work at Polyglot Chemicals, where Gabriel Trumpet was just promoted from being our top salesperson to the worst sales manager you can imagine." A nurse once asked, "Have you been studying Central Hospital? They promoted Dr. Nostrum, a very good physician, to director. He has exchanged the practice of medicine for the practice of mismanagement." An air force officer expressed concern about my knowledge of mil-

itary protocol and procedures. And so it went at each lecture—
I was talking about the education system and listeners thought I
was describing their organizations.

A Universal Phenomenon

Naturally, I wondered if every hierarchy functioned like the
school system, so I looked further afield. The results were most
revealing. On a visit to the public library I noticed that all the
books on pregnancy were on a shelf next to the floor where the
people who needed them most probably couldn't see them. I ordered a book about incompetence in business from a large publishing house. Two weeks later I received a letter which said in
part: "We thank you for your recent order and wish we could
fill it at once, but improvements in our procedures will mean a
delay in shipping." I read a book, *The Wastemakers* by Vance
Packard, about manufacturers deliberately making products that
wouldn't last. Before I finished reading the book, the binding
disintegrated and the pages fell out.

I interviewed executives, within and outside the educational
establishment, about their promotion policies. Cap Preece, a
school superintendent, put it most succinctly when he said,
"Anyone who is competent is eligible for promotion." Each executive I interviewed agreed that competence should be rewarded by promotion and that incompetence should be a bar to
promotion. None seemed to understand that in a system where
competence constituted eligibility and incompetence constituted
a bar to promotion, each individual would eventually come to
rest at a level of incompetence.

Higher up the Hierarchy

In 1964, I became a professor of education at the University
of British Columbia, where I taught what I had learned about
teacher competence. This small beginning evolved into a ten-
year teacher competency program, which I completed at the

University of Southern California. It was my main professional interest until I retired.

While at the University of British Columbia, I attended a one-act play festival at Vancouver's Metro Theatre. The setting for one play was a sinking ship which had hit a reef in a storm. The actors were required to lurch about the stage in unison to create the illusion of the ship's listing. The actor playing the lead persisted in turning his back on the audience and lurching in the direction opposite to the other players. He also made what appeared to be irrelevant gestures into the wings. During the intermission that followed, I met a friend, the playwright Raymond Hull. When I asked him if he knew anything about the strange performance we had just witnessed, he said, "Yes. The man playing the lead is really quite a good actor. The problem is that he wrote this impossible play and is directing it as well as acting in it. Sometimes he forgets he is acting and turns his back on the audience to direct his cast. The strange gestures are signals to the electrician and stagehands in the wings."

"He is a victim of the Peter Principle," I said: "A competent actor who has risen to his level of incompetence as a playwright and director." Ray seemed fascinated by the idea and claimed that I had given meaning to all the incompetence he had been encountering.

In the Introduction to the book *The Peter Principle,* Ray describes his response to my explanation.

The intermission was too short for him to do more than whet my curiosity. After the show I went to his home and sat till 3:00 A.M. listening to his lucid, startlingly original exposition of a theory that at last answered my question, "Why incompetence?" Dr. Peter exonerated Adam, agitators, and accident, and arraigned one feature of our society as the perpetrator and rewarder of incompetence.

Ray was insistent I should write a book about my discovery, but I declined because I was deep into my education project and was completing a textbook on how to translate medical, psychological, and social-work diagnoses into educational implementation.* Ray stressed society's need for a Peter Principle book and suggested we collaborate in its writing. I agreed and gave him my files on incompetence, my lecture notes, and my writings on the subject. Ray and I met frequently over the next year as we worked on the book. When we were satisfied that our manuscript said exactly what we wanted to say, I submitted it to a major publisher.

Peter Principle Victim

The first rejection letter stated, in part:

> I regret to say that I can foresee no commercial possibilities for such a book, and consequently can offer you no encouragement in this connection. I don't think the book would appeal in any way to our Trade or Paperback Divisions; nor can I foresee sufficient inter-divisional sales potential for this project to warrant publication by a commercial publisher.

Over the next few years the manuscript was submitted to thirteen publishers. Some of the rejection slips were form letters, but some editors took time to explain why the book was unsatisfactory. One said, "You should not deal so lightly with a serious topic." Another suggested, "If you are writing a comedy, it should not contain so many tragic case studies." Still another said, "I will reconsider publication if you will make up your mind and rewrite it as a humorous book or as a serious scientific work." An editor who liked the book submitted it to his company's editorial board. He reported to me that the board could not decide how to classify the book and so rejected it.

When asked about the manuscript, I claimed it was satire.

*Laurence J. Peter, *Prescriptive Teaching* (New York: McGraw-Hill, 1965).

The usual response was: "I don't think it's satire. I think you are serious." I was disturbed to find so many persons in publishing who didn't know about literary satire. I explained that satire was a form of writing in which the message is serious and the method is humor. The objective is to tell the truth in a funny way. My attempts at an explanation didn't seem to help. I recall one editor who, after patiently listening to my explanation, shook his head and said, "That's academic. What I want to know is, are you serious or not?" He was beyond my help.

Because publishers were not ready for the book, we decided to write some Peter Principle articles and see what the response would be. The articles published in Esquire and other national magazines were well received.

Soon after I moved to Los Angeles, Marshall Lumsden, an editor at the *Los Angeles Times,* read some of my articles and requested that I write one for the paper. I wrote about the Los Angeles zoo that had just been built. Alterations costing hundreds of thouands of dollars were required before the zoo could be opened. A hazardous pedestrian bridge over the rhinoceros pen had to be removed at a cost of many thousands. The moat around the lions' den was so narrow the lions could escape. It seemed they were trying to run the zoo on the honor system. With the zoo's many flaws the story made an excellent Peter Principle example. The *Times* received more than four hundred letters praising the article. One of those who heard about it was Lawrence Hughes, president of William Morrow and Company. He asked me if I had thought of writing a book about the Peter Principle, so when one of his editors came to California, I dusted off the old manuscript and let the editor read it.

The book, released in February 1969, climbed by late July to the number one position on *The New York Times* nonfiction best-seller list, where it remained for six months, followed by months as the mass-market paperback best seller. It was translated and published in thirty-seven foreign editions, becoming an international best seller. Both *The Wall Street Journal* and the Socialist Labor Party of America praised the book, and it was eagerly read in both capitalist and communist countries. It inspired a number of serious research projects and each study supported the correctness of my observations.

Principle Solves Problems

The success of the book resolved three major problems for me. First, my educational research had reached a stage where I needed help. My center for teaching handicapped children was equipped so that my associates and I could observe teacher-pupil interaction in a precise manner, and record and reinforce those teacher behaviors that were effective. I was supporting this operation and my research myself, but these projects had reached a point where they needed funding beyond my means. I realized I had reached my level of incompetence as a fund raiser when all my requests from government agencies and private foundations were rejected. The royalties from *The Peter Principle* enabled me to complete the research.

Second, in attempting to stay at my level of competence, I had carried creative incompetence about as far as I dared. After *The Peter Principle* was published I received no more offers of promotion. The administrators did not want someone among them who did not take them seriously. Apparently the book was the ultimate in creative incompetence. When in 1974, I left the educational establishment, they didn't even give me a testimonial coffee break. It is understandable. Since then I have worked in blissful independence of hierarchal responsibilities and restrictions.

Although the principle had helped me in many ways, I was not immune to its influence. When I retired we moved to a small, older house out near the ocean. It was badly in need of repair. One problem was a window in my office that was stuck completely shut. I had the carpenter repair it and replace the sill. When he was finished, the window would open but the lights wouldn't work. The electrician discovered a nail had been driven through a cable, causing a short. He repaired the cable and the lights worked, but later I discovered that in nailing the trim back on the window, he had started a crack in a pane of glass. The glazier replaced the glass and then I had the painter finish the job. I declared the project complete when I found that he had painted the window shut and I couldn't get it open.

A NEW SCIENCE

Through my investigations of promotions within organizations, I came to realize that the study of hierarchies was in reality a new science. I called it *hierarchiology*. Since we go to school, work in, and are governed by hierarchies, understanding this newest of the social sciences is important to you. The balance of this book is devoted to my hierarchiological studies.

> **PE'TER PRIN'CIPLE,** any of several satirical "laws" concerning organizational structure, especially one which holds that people tend to be promoted till they reach a level beyond their competence [from the title of a book by Laurence J. Peter (b. 1919), Canadian educator].
> —*The Random House College Dictionary,* 1979

2

Law and Disorder

The law, in its majestic equality, forbids all men to sleep under bridges, to bed in the streets, and to steal bread—the rich as well as the poor.   —ANATOLE FRANCE

There are two kinds of laws that apply to the human condition. First there are the axioms, rules, theories, proverbs, and principles that describe human behavior.

> *Ade's Law:* Anyone can win, unless there happens to be a second entry.
> *Rogin's Rule:* You can always get more of what you don't need—including poverty.
> *Barnum's Theory:* If you can fool all of the people some of the time, that's enough.

Such laws are intended to help us cope with the perplexity of human society and the perversity of nature. The second variety of laws are those legal statutes enforced by authority to place reasonable limitations on the behavior of people in a community or country.

TRANSCENDING LAWS

From 1970 until the present, a profusion of laws has been published in an attempt to help us laugh at or cope with the foibles, blunders, delays, maladroitness, and general confusion of contemporary society. Although many of these laws are based on accurate observations and are expressed with wit, the three best known were developed before 1970: Murphy's Law, Parkinson's Law, and the Peter Principle.

It all began back in 1949, when air force Captain Edward A. Murphy, Jr., a development engineer at Wright Field Aircraft Lab, designed a harness to be worn by a test pilot to measure how much acceleration the human body could withstand. The transducer device was fitted with sixteen sensors to measure the strain. Here is Ed Murphy's own description of what happened:

> I thought I had succeeded and sent my transducer to Edwards Air Force Base at Muroc, where the Air Force was conducting experimental crash research. There they installed my transducer on a rocket sled ridden by John Paul Stapp, a major back then, who later became known as "the fastest man on earth" for having ridden a rocket sled going over 600 mph.
>
> The next thing I heard was that the test had failed, and my transducer was being blamed for it. Because it was a very expensive failure, I felt it was in my best interest to examine the results personally at Edwards and hopefully clear both my name and transducer.

Murphy went on to say that he believed the problem was the way a strain gauge had been wired, causing his transducer to malfunction. "There are only two ways to wire a strain gauge," he said: "the right way and 90 degrees from the right way."

Murphy's investigation found that the gauge was wired, as he suspected, the wrong way. That caused him to make a remark to the effect that if there is any way for the technician to do it wrong, he will.

George E. Nichols, a project manager for Northrop who happened to be present when Murphy uttered these words, dubbed

Whatever can go wrong will go wrong.

the remark Murphy's Law. References to Murphy's Law in technical publications popularized the concept and helped perpetuate it throughout the English-speaking world. Today, Murphy's Law is applied to virtually every field of human endeavor where there's concern for reliability.

Probably because Edward Murphy did not write his law, but only inspired it by his remark, it has assumed a variety of wordings over the years. The best-known version is:

Murphy's Law: Whatever can go wrong will go wrong.

Today, Murphy works as a reliability engineer for Hughes Helicopter, Inc., and seems quietly amused by all the books and calendars that have exploited his idea and have never earned him a cent.

In a recent conversation Ed Murphy explained to me that he was completely serious when he made his pronouncement. He intended it as a warning to machine designers and engineers to plan equipment with safety in mind, so that it will be difficult, if not impossible, to operate the equipment the wrong way. He also stated most emphatically that what he really said in summarizing the event that day, and what he regards as Murphy's Law, was: "If there are two or more ways to do something, and one of those ways can result in a catastrophe, then someone will do it that way." Even Murphy's Law was a victim of Murphy's Law.

On November 19, 1955, Professor C. Northcote Parkinson published an article in the staid pages of *The Economist* of London about a law he had discovered while investigating the British Admiralty and the Colonial Office.

Parkinson's Law: Work expands to fill the time available for its completion.

The basic truth of his law was instantly acknowledged. In 1957, when his first book on the subject was published, Parkinson's Law reached a larger audience. Its worldwide implications for all bureaucracies were generally accepted without reservations.

In describing his discovery, Parkinson explained he was a professor of history at the University of Malaysia at the time that the British colony was preparing to become an independent country. This meant it had to have a new radio network, a new university, and a new history curriculum. Before long Parkinson found himself on thirty-two committees. During this period he made many of his observations about committees. One of his discoveries about committee size supported the old rhyme:

> Committees of twenty deliberate plenty,
> Committees of ten act now and then,
> But most jobs are done by committees of one.

As he studied Malaysian bureaucracy in action he recalled his experience as a staff officer in the army during World War

II. He had observed that in wartime a whole organizational structure could be built in two weeks that would take years to accumulate in peacetime. A wartime bureaucracy can begin, grow, and proliferate so quickly that the entire process is evident and available for easy study.

Parkinson provided as an example the case of the private asked to interpret aerial photographs. Two days later he was back, complaining that he needed another man to help him, as there were too many photographs. He also requested a promotion to lance corporal in order to have authority over his helper. These reasonable requests were granted, and in three months he had a staff of eighty-five and had become a lieutenant colonel who never looked at another aerial photograph because he was too busy tending to administration.

Parkinson deduced his law from two accurate observations of the civil service: (1) An official wants to multiply subordinates, not rivals, and (2) officials make work for each other.

Stan Patt, a typical bureaucrat, thinking himself over-worked, hired not one assistant—who might become his successor—but two subordinates, Bea Guile and Sue Port. By dividing the work so that he would be the only one who comprehended both jobs, he protected his position. As these employees made work for each other, Bea Guile found herself overworked and demanded two assistants of her own. Stan Patt could avoid internal friction only by recommending two assistants also for Sue Port. Seven officials were then doing what one did before. The seven made so much work for each other that all were fully occupied and Stan Patt was actually busier than ever.

Parkinson's Law predicts the ever-rising pyramid of government bureaucracy and the inevitability of staff growth whether there is more work, less work, or no work at all.

I met C. Northcote Parkinson only once, but during our brief conversation I was impressed with his understanding of the organization of committees, of how they are conceived through the pollination of a simple idea, and how the seed of a concept then sprouts and grows like a tree, develops branches, bears fruit, drops its seed, and starts a whole new generation of committees. One thing was clear to me: Parkinson's Law was the product of careful observation distilled through the process of of a creative mind.

What have Murphy's Law, Parkinson's Law, and the Peter Principle in common? They emerged from careful observation of real events and provided a generalization giving those events new meaning. Why did these laws catch on? Each one encapsulated a part of the complexity of human experience, and stated it in a brief, understandable, and memorable sentence. Why were they universally accepted? Each was a basic truth that was valid worldwide, regardless of political system, religious belief, or racial difference—laws that transcend all national and cultural boundaries.

Mirror, Mirror on the Wall

The only complete map of the world is the world itself, and yet a simplification in the form of a globe or a road map can be most helpful. Likewise, I do not think the Peter Principle has to explain everything in order to provide us with useful insights or practical guidance.

On occasion I have caught a glimpse of myself in a mirror and, not immediately recognizing myself, begun to laugh before realizing what I was doing. Often it is in such moments that true progress toward self-understanding has occurred. The Peter Principle is a mirror of human fallibility. In a moment of amusement we may glimpse ourselves reflected and see that our aspirations are probably leading to incompetence rather than fulfillment. When a law functions so as to cause us to pause, reflect, and consider alternatives, it goes beyond explanation of what has happened, sheds lights on the future, and influences what is to be.

Corollaries

A corollary is a deduction or inference that follows a main proposition. The value of corollaries to the Peter Principle is that they may lead us to consider more consequences or applications of the major concept. A small sample follows, with the rest of the corollaries appearing throughout the book.

COROLLARY 1: The cream rises until it sours.

COROLLARY 2: For every job in the world there is someone, somewhere, who can't do it. Given enough promotions, that someone will get the job.

COROLLARY 3: A journey of one thousand miles ends with but a single step.

COROLLARY 4: All useful work is done by those who have not yet reached their level of incompetence.

THE LAW OF THE LAND

As the Peter Principle invades our major institutions, and more persons arrive at their levels of incompetence, the need for regulation escalates. A group of capable individuals needs only general guidelines and clearly stated objectives in order to function competently. Inept employees require rules limiting their actions. Rules will not produce competence but they will protect the hierarchy even as regulations proliferate into their own complex hierarchy of incompetence. This occurs when the simplest task becomes so encumbered with regulation that its accomplishment is next to impossible.

The job of changing an incorrect zip code number would, at first glance, appear to be a simple matter of crossing out the wrong number and replacing it with the correct one. In Washington they see things differently. The Federal Communications Commis-

Inept employers require rules limiting their actions.

sion's instruction for correction of a zip code error was as follows:

> 1. The U.S. Department of Commerce, Environmental Research Laboratories, has notified the commission that the zip code for its facilities at Boulder, Colo., is not correctly printed in sections 73.711, 73.1030 and 74.12 of the commission's rules.
> 2. The city address zip code in sections 73.711 (c) (2), 73.1030 (b) (2) and 74.12 (c) (2) is corrected to read as follows: Boulder Colorado 80303.
> 3. We conclude that adoption of the editorial amendment shown in this order will serve the public interest. Prior notice of rule making, effective date provisions and public procedure thereon are unnecessary, pursuant to the administrative procedure and judicial review provisions of 5 U.S.C. 533 (b) (3) (B), inasmuch as this amendment imposes no additional burdens and raises no issue upon which comments would serve any useful purpose.
> 4. Therefore, it is ordered that, pursuant to sections 4 (1), 303 (4) and 5 (a) (1) of the Communications Act of 1934, as amended, and section 0.281 of the commission's rules and regulations, is amended as set forth in paragraph 2 above, effective Nov. 10, 1978.

We have excelled in the escalation of quantity over quality in the creation of laws. Whenever a special-interest group believes there is an evil that can be handled by legislation, we are in danger of having a complicated and elaborate statute devised. The motivation may be good but the tendency is not toward organization and clarity but toward piling on more and more complexity—and in some cases absurdity.

> Laws are made to trouble people, and the more trouble they make, the longer they stay on the statute books.   —FINLEY PETER DUNNE

It's the Law

Form F4473 is used by the Department of the Treasury, Bureau of Alcohol, Tobacco and Firearms to record sale of a gun. Section A, to be completed personally by the purchaser, asks: "Are you a fugitive from justice?"

> To make crime unprofitable, let the government run it.   —IRENE PETER

In Colorado, the maximum penalty for destroying a house with fire is twenty years, but with explosives, only ten years. The maximum sentence for stealing a dog is ten years, but the sentence for killing a dog is six months or a $500 fine.

A Mohave County, Arizona, law decrees that anyone caught stealing soap must wash himself with it until it is all used up.

The village of Lakefield, Ontario, passed noise-abatement legislation which permitted birds to sing for thirty minutes during the day and fifteen minutes at night. The city council clerk who wrote the legislation, Earl Cuddie, was flooded with calls from all over Canada asking how he would get the birds to stop singing. Cuddie admitted, "I guess I drafted the law in such a hurry I just didn't stop to think."

The Arkansas legislature enacted a law stating that the Arkansas River can rise no farther than to the Main Street bridge in Little Rock.

A New Jersey Superior Court ruled that a night watchman can be eligible for overtime pay while sleeping on the job.

According to a law in Danville, Pennsylvania, fire hydrants must be checked one hour before all fires.

An Oklahoma law states that the drivers of "any vehicle involved in an accident resulting in death . . . shall immediately stop . . . and give his name and address to the person struck."

> The first my client knew of the accident was when it occurred.   —A lawyer defending his client

In Seattle it is unlawful to carry a concealed weapon that is over six feet in length.

Watering your lawn while it is raining is against the law in Holyoke, Massachusetts.

San Francisco has an ordinance which bans picking up used confetti to throw over again.

The 1930 Virginia Penal Code prohibits "corrupt practices or bribery by any person other than candidates."

And, within the city limits of Quitman, Georgia, it is unlawful for any chicken to cross any road.

Law Enforcement

The law may be imperfectly written and be riddled with loopholes but sometimes the way it is enforced runs a close second for incompetency and occasionally for humor.

A newspaper item announced that three bicycles had been stolen from Exeter Street. The police were quoted as saying they believe a bicycle thief is at work.

In the summer of 1982 six Chicago police officers were arrested for selling heroin out of their squad cars while on duty.

In 1980 the warden of England's Featherstone Prison granted permission for the prisoners to take up pottery-making. The prisoners counterfeited the work of master potter Bernard Leach, even matching rare glazes. The pieces were smuggled out of the prison and sold for over £1,000 each at such prestigious galleries as Sotheby's and Christie's. The fraud was discovered when suspicion was aroused by so many "new" Leaches.

COROLLARY 5: Competence always contains the seeds of incompetence.

In Saginaw, Michigan, a man was pulled over for a driving violation. When the officers searched his car they found a revolver, so they arrested him. They had to release him the next day with an apology. The revolver had fallen out of the policeman's holster while he was searching the car.

I'm not against the police; I'm just afraid of them.
—ALFRED HITCHCOCK

A convicted drug dealer in Minneapolis deducted the cost of buying amphetamines, cocaine, and marijuana on his income tax return. Jeffrey Edmonson also deducted as business expenses telephone, transportation, apartment rent, packaging materials, and the scale he used to weigh his contraband. IRS officials told him he couldn't deduct criminal business expenses, but Edmondson took them to court and won. U.S. Tax Court Judge William Goffe ruled the expenses were ordinary and necessary and allowed the deductions.

A district court in California threw out the arrest of Hector Solario, even though arresting officers saw him stuffing jewelry in a sack during a burglary. The court held that the police should have stopped at the open door, knocked, and identified themselves before entering to arrest the trespassing felon for burglary in progress.

Burglary charges against nineteen-year-old Michael Moran were dropped. His father, Lieutenant Junice Moran, had searched the boy's room and found a stereo believed to have been stolen in a recent burglary. Lieutenant Moran confronted his son with the stereo and the son admitted to the break-in. The Indianana superior court ruled that the boy's rights had been violated and dismissed the case.

> When constabulary duty's to be done,
> The policeman's lot is not a happy one.
> —W. S. GILBERT

By 1980 the three-year-old Cuyahoga County jail in Ohio was overflowing. The jail was originally designed to hold 1,200 prisoners but when completed could only hold 800. As the cost of the justice center—which included police facilities and courtrooms—skyrocketed from $61 million to $135 million, the size of the jail shrank. Deputies were told not to look for any of the 4,982 fugitives wanted on felony charges, as the jail could not accommodate them.

Crime will be committed as long as criminals aren't.
—BILL DANA

Harry Seigler, on trial for robbery and murder, became nervous while awaiting the jury's verdict. The accused, a three-time loser on previous robbery charges, copped a plea of guilty in exchange for a sixty-year sentence with twenty years suspended. The judge kept the jury waiting while he accepted the deal. When he informed the jury of the guilty plea, the jurors moaned. They had already reached their verdict: not guilty.

The defendant appeared in a Pontiac, Michigan, court without a lawyer to represent him. The judge announced that he would serve as defense counsel, presented an argument on his client's behalf, then ruled that the defendant was guilty as charged.

Frank Wills, the security guard who discovered the Watergate break-in, is serving time for shoplifting. The unemployed Wills was living with his mother in South Carolina and shoplifted a $15 pair of sneakers as a gift for his son. Unlike the convicted Watergate criminals, Wills got the maximum sentence—twelve months.

These are the terms (though their original sentences may have been longer) actually served by the Watergate bunch: G. Gordon Liddy, fifty-two months; E. Howard Hunt, Jr., John N. Mitchell, H. R. Haldeman, and John D. Ehrlichman, twelve months; Dwight L. Chapin, eight months; Charles W. Colson and Jeb Stuart Magruder, seven months; Herbert W. Kalmbach, six months; John W. Dean, III, under five months; Egil Krogh, Jr., and Donald H. Segretti, four months; Richard M. Nixon, full pardon.

The accomplice of corruption is frequently our own indifference.   —BESS MYERSON

Portugese Army officials were investigating the death of a twelve-year-old boy who was shot by a sentry. The sentry claimed the boy ignored his challenge in the dark and proceeded. In the trial, the court decided to reconstruct the incident. The thirty-three-year-old civilian playing the part of the boy was also shot dead.

> The policeman isn't there to create disorder; the policeman is there to preserve disorder.
> —RICHARD J. DALEY, Chicago mayor

Forty-eight of the fifty-four physicians, psychiatrists, and dentists employed at Rikers Island prison in New York were charged with falsifying their time cards, travel time, and reimbursements.

> White collar crime, that is crime in the suites, is as destructive as crime in the street.   —MEG STAAHL

A member of the press asked Police Chief John B. Layton of the District of Columbia what accounted for the rash of weekend robberies. Layton replied, "The biggest factor is the inclination of certain individuals for acquiring funds by illegal means."

> You can get much further with a kind word and a gun than you can with a kind word alone.
> —AL CAPONE

Twenty-five-year-old Michael James of Chippewa Falls, Wisconsin, told a judge he would not accept a job as part of his sentence because the job the court offered paid $350 per month, less than the $300 James received from county assistance combined with his $130 in food stamps.

In Brisbane, Australia, Peter Stocker pleaded guilty to stealing twenty-five front doors from various residences. The unem-

We must not assume they would enter a life of crime intending to get caught.

ployed carpenter was convicted, fined, and ordered to return the doors to their rightful owners. Eleven of the doors, however, had never been reported missing. The alert public prosecutor issued the following request to locals: "If you see a house without a door, please draw this to the attention of the householder."

> We don't seem able to check crime, so why not legalize it and then tax it out of business.
> —WILL ROGERS

Crime Doesn't Pay

The above examples lead one to assume that these lawmakers and law enforcers intended to be effective, but that when they perpetrated these fiascoes they were functioning at their levels of incompetence. Similarly, as we turn our attention to the lawbreakers, we must not assume they would enter a life of crime intending to get caught. We must hypothesize that most who become criminals do so with the highest resolve of being successful.

Of course, in crime, as in other high-risk professions, anxiety can be a contributing factor in the creation of blunders, and, as in all human enterprise, there are those few who at a subconscious level have a compulsion to fail. But the dynamics of success and failure remain the same for law enforcer and lawbreaker.

> Crime doesn't pay; sooner or later every criminal gets
> a parking ticket.   —Ted Zeigler

Kammy Jean Sullivan of Spring Valley, California, changed her plea in a car-theft case from innocent to guilty after the car owner identified the jacket Sullivan was wearing at the trial as one of the stolen items.

A thief was arrested outside a London meat market. The officer noticed the man couldn't stop shivering and further investigation revealed why: The thief had a frozen sirloin of beef inside his pants.

A bank robber in Portland, Oregon, passed a note to the teller: "This is a hold-up and I've got a gun." The teller waited and the robber wrote further: "Put all the money in a paper bag." The cashier wrote on the bottom of the paper: "I don't have a paper bag." The robber left the bank.

Carrying $1,710 in cash, accused robbery suspect Oliver Paxton ran out of the Community Bank of East Los Angeles to find he had locked his keys in the car.

A shoplifter in Barnsley, England, was simultaneously apprehended by four store detectives. On that day the store was hosting a convention of store detectives.

In a Southhampton supermarket a thief wheeled his loaded cart to the checkout stand. When the bill was rung up, the man proffered a £10 note. The cashier opened the drawer, and the thief grabbed the drawer's contents and bolted. The drawer contained £4 and 37 pence. The cashier was still holding the £10 note.

Arthur Gertsen, a convicted con man, was being held in lieu of $31,000 bond on charges of forgery, bounced checks, and parole violations when he was brought before the judge again. He was caught offering people a chance to make 128 percent annual interest by borrowing money on the equity in their homes. He made the calls on the jailhouse phone. A judge increased his bail to $100,000 and revoked his telephone privileges.

Thomas F. Richardson was a member of the gang that committed the famed Brink's robbery, one of the biggest in U.S. history—$2.8 million, $1.2 million in currency. Shortly before his death he calculated that including the preparation time for the heist and his time in prison (more than thirty years), his share of the take amounted to about $1.25 per hour.

An accused burglar in San Antonio fled from the courtroom in an escape attempt. Hoping to get lost in the crowd, he joined a passing pack of joggers—all members of the police SWAT team.

In Riverside, California, a man held up a doughnut shop wearing a pillowcase over his head. The armed robber took $60 from the cashier. Because he had forgotten to cut eyeholes, he had to lift the corner of the pillowcase to find the door. A customer in the shop recognized him and he was arrested at his nearby home.

When the parking-meter bandit went to bail out a friend, he was apprehended. He paid the $860 bail in nickels and dimes.

Sacramento, California: Police Sergeant Melvin Chuckovich told a thief: "You should be ashamed of yourself, stealing those bicycles from children.'' Some time later Chuckovich saw the man in handcuffs at the police station. He said, ''I took your advice. I've been stealing cars.''

A man wanted in New York City in connection with a larceny case was caught after a lengthy manhunt. He was working as a cafeteria dishwasher in the identification division of FBI headquarters in Washington, D.C.

A New York City office-supply firm installed a new phone-call accounting system. After a weekend burglary was discovered, an employee happened to notice that a call appeared on the report at a time when the plant was closed. The burglar was caught—he had phoned home.

D. B. Cooper became infamous when he hijacked a Northwest Orient jet on a flight from Portland to Seattle in 1971. He demanded $200,000 and four parachutes and made his escape while the Boeing 727 was still in flight. Within a year twenty-one copycats attempted the same thing; none succeeded. Sixteen were sentenced to prison, two were committed to mental institutions, and three died in the attempt.

At Northern Mexico's Saltillo Prison, several convicts spent five months digging a tunnel to freedom. A parade of seventy-five convicts burst through the floor at the end of the tunnel—into the courtroom where most of them had been sentenced. They were returned to their cells and the surprised magistrate added time to their sentences.

J. Ealey committed a burglary in Detroit, but accidentally left his dog at the scene of the crime. The alarms brought the police, who found the dog. Shouting, ''Home, boy!'' they followed the dog and arrived only seconds after the returning burglar.

> If crime doesn't pay, how come it's one of our biggest businesses? —MITCHELL GORDON

Incompetence can occur when the tools for the job are not of top quality, as demonstrated in this case: The Covina, California, police reported that two young men—Victor Cross, twenty-one, and Herbert Taylor, twenty-six—decided to try their hand at robbery. They equipped themselves with the tools of the trade: a paper sack for the loot, a mask to hide the face, and a shotgun to expedite the transaction.

The enterprise was well planned. One entered the Playtime Liquors store in Covina wearing the mask, carrying the gun and loot sack, and the other stayed in the getaway car in the parking lot. All went well up to a point. The clerk put $180 in coins and small bills in the sack. The holdup man headed for the getaway car, but the loot sack split, spilling its contents. Then the butt of the shotgun fell off and the string broke on the mask and it, too, fell off.

They still managed to escape, but were arrested ninety minutes later when they returned to the scene of the crime, apparently to look for the butt of the gun.

COROLLARY 6: Incompetence plus incompetence equals incompetence.

3

A Clot for Every Slot

An excellent plumber is infinitely more admirable than an
incompetent philosopher. The society which scorns excel-
lence in plumbing because plumbing is a humble activity
and tolerates shoddiness in philosophy because it is an ex-
alted activity will have neither good plumbing nor good
philosophy. Neither its pipes nor its theories will hold
water.   —JOHN GARDNER

Competence is defined as the state of being capable, but in op-
erational terms it must be described as the possession of abilities
or skills required to perform a specific function. The competent
salesperson must be able to sell merchandise. The competent
doctor must be able to provide patients with beneficial medical
services. The competent mechanic should be able to return your
car in better operating condition than when you took it in. Although the skills of the sales representative, the doctor, and the
mechanic are different, each is competent to the degree that performance meets output criteria appropriate for his or her profession.

The observation or measurement of output is the only scientific way to evaluate competence, and yet there is a tendency
to view competence in relation to input. Weight may be given
to the opinion of a professor with a Ph.D., when in fact he may
be an educated fool. His ideas are valued for his effort in acquiring an education and climbing the academic ladder to full
professor, rather than for the relevance and quality of his thoughts.
Input is an important consideration, but competence can only be

The competent salesperson must be able to sell merchandise.

measured as output. Frequently the individual who is highly qualified by education and experience is also highly competent, but one should be careful not to expect automatically that those with the most input will always produce the best output.

COROLLARY 7: Whenever something is worth doing, it is worth finding someone competent to do it.

AN EXACT SCIENCE

Hierarchiology is the science that attempts, through objective study, to provide a deeper understanding of the structure of human organizations. Examination of the case histories and examples provided in this book will reveal the nature of society's hierarchal structure so that what at first may appear to be a chaotic mass of unrelated information takes on meaning. It is through our understanding of social organization, and how the Peter Principle operates within it, that human society becomes intelligible.

In our scientific study of hierarchies we must avoid being moralistic concerning competence and incompetence; we should not assume that inept individuals are lacking in a desire to be virtuous or productive. My interviews, while providing mainly subjective information, indicated that those who met the objective criteria qualifying them as incompetent would like to be more productive. Each employee expressed a definite wish to be more useful if he or she could. Further, most incompetents realized, in a vague sort of way, that the failure of the company would leave them jobless, or the collapse of society would leave them stranded.

COROLLARY 8: In a hierarchy, accomplishment is inversely proportional to its height.

While scientific rigor requires that individual capability be evaluated in terms of objective, observable, or measurable output, it must not be overlooked that both competence and incompetence can be functions of almost any aspect of the human personality.

MULTICAUSAL INCOMPETENCE FILE, CASE NO. 7

This case study is presented to illustrate the variety of human characteristics that can, under the relevant conditions, become disabilities.

Professional

In thirty-five years at Akme Lead Weight and Sinker, Inc., Jerry Attrick had risen from lead-ingot handler to general manager. He had firsthand experience in every process of the production of Akme products and was capable of managing and maintaining the plant's operation and its system of distribution. Unfortunately for Jerry, the board of directors decided to acquire the interests of another company, Perfect Pitch Pewter Tuning Forks, and to combine the operations of the two companies under Jerry's management. Jerry was apprehensive from the start. He knew the lead business from actual experience, but pewter was a whole new world to him. Distribution of weights and tuning forks involved drastically different procedures. Jerry Attrick was too old and set in his ways to accommodate the new techniques required for managing the complex business of the new corporate enterprise, Akme Lead and Pewter Products, Inc. Jerry Attrick was at his level of incompetence because he lacked the professional capability required by the position he now occupied.

Physical

The amalgamation of Akme Lead and Perfect Pitch required some major changes in order to create the new administrative structure. Ann Jyna was promoted from secretary to office manager. She was eager for the increased responsibility and substantial salary increase accompanying it. Although she was technically

competent, the strain of the increased responsibility and complexity of her job began to take its toll. It began with tension
headaches and crippling lower-back pain. When she went for a
checkup, because of chest pains, the doctor was surprised to
discover that her blood pressure was dangerously high.

In spite of Ann Jyna's ability to perform her job competently, physically she was not capable of adapting to the stress
it generated which progressively increased her time off the job.
She had reached her level of physical or biological incompetence.

Mental

As foreman, Stu Pidd was popular with Akme workers down
on the lead casting floor. He was a pleasant, kindly person who
knew the job of lead molding from his years of experience. He
was conscientious and turned out exactly the number of quality
lead castings ordered.

With the Lead-Pewter merger, Stu was promoted to molding
supervisor, and when he received orders for lead and pewter
castings, he had to make decisions about allocations of both
workers and equipment. This new responsibility taxed his
decision-making ability. Instead of simple orders, he received
guidelines and policy statements from management. He lacked
the intellectual capacity to deal effectively with abstractions. He
habitually misinterpreted company policy and made illogical decisions, reducing the efficiency of the molding department. Stu
Pidd had reached his level of incompetence through mental inadequacy.

Social

Cal Luss, a recent graduate in metallurgical engineering who
had been in charge of alloying the tin, antimony, copper, and
lead at Perfect Pitch Pewter, was promoted to manager of the
total metals operation for the new corporation. He was dedi-

cated and completely serious about his work. Cal, who had been a good metals man, now had to work with people. An an engineer he was competent at working with materials, but as a manager he was incompetent at achieving good results with people. He was solemn and completely humorless in all his dealings with personnel. He was an expert at metallurgy formulae, but he had no equivalent people formulae. He could not make personnel decisions by using his calculator or through computer readouts. In his frustration he usually made unwise people-decisions. Cal Luss, a competent engineer, had reached his level of incompetence through his inability to relate to people.

Emotional

Hy Sterik was an enthusiastic and talented commercial illustrator in the advertising department at Perfect Pitch Pewter at the time of the merger. In his new position as advertising director for Akme Products he vacillated from heights of enthusiasm to depths of despair. His dedication to production of beautiful ads, which worked so well with the artistic consumers in the tuning-fork market, was not sufficiently appreciated in the lead-weight and sinker business. His preferential treatment of those on the tuning-fork side of the business, and his snubbing of those in the lead-weight business, caused strife within the company. He became tense and jittery, short-tempered and subject to emotional outbursts. When his tuning-fork ads were appreciated he was euphoric, and when his sinker ads were criticized he was often in tears. His feelings clouded his reasoning and controlled his every move. He was at his level of emotional incompetence.

Ethical

Mal Larky had been the top sales rep at Akme. His breezy manner, risqué jokes, and tall tales were popular with his lead-weight customers. He was pragmatic in his use of the truth in that he scrupulously avoided it, except when it served his purpose. His customers didn't take his exaggeration of his products' virtues very seriously, and furthermore it didn't matter much because there wasn't much competition to speak of in the lead-weight business.

When he was promoted to sales manager of Akme Lead and Pewter, it became obvious that his sales methods were not an asset in management. He made promises to individual salespersons regarding territories, advertising support, and personal help that he never fulfilled. He used underhanded and dishonest methods of manipulation in working with his staff. He advised his tuning-fork salespersons to employ his methods of exaggeration in promoting sales. When they tried his sales technique, customers turned to other brands, of which there were many. Through his dishonesty, Mal Larky had reached his level of ethical incompetency.

ASSETS TO LIABILITIES

The most obvious incompetence is when individuals cannot do their jobs—when, like Jerry Attrick, they lack the professional capability to handle expanded responsibilities. But many other hidden weaknesses can reveal themselves as incompetence when individuals are raised to the appropriate level. Almost any human characteristic, even those viewed as assets at one stage, can when escalated to a sufficient height, constitute incompetence. An asset at one level may be a liability at another.

While in high school, Richard M. Nixon began his spectacular career working for two summer vacations in Prescott, Arizona, as a slick and persuasive barker for the wheel-of-chance at the Slippery Gulch Rodeo. At Whittier College he continued to develop his ability to persuade others through public speaking when he became leader of the debate team.

In late 1945, in Whittier, California, Nixon appeared before the Republican Committee of 100 and gave his first political speech. In a talk that lasted only ten minutes, he displayed his genius for political rhetoric. He spoke of the American system as consisting of two ideas. One "advocated by the New Deal," he said, "is government control in regulating our lives. The other calls for individual freedoms and all that initiative can produce. I hold with the latter viewpoint. I believe that returning veterans—and I have talked to many of them in the foxholes—will not be satisfied with a dole or a government handout." This speech was exactly what the committee wanted to hear. The Committee of 100 voted unanimously to make him the congressional nominee. In this speech his technique of persuasion was revealed. He could present attractively and palatably that which was untrue. There is no record of Nixon's having ever been near a foxhole during his navy service in the rear echelons of the Pacific, nor is it probable that those in the foxholes were preoccupied with conflicting economic philosophies.

His feet were set on the path he would follow for the next twenty-nine years. In his 1946 campaign for Congress he defeated his opponent, Jerry Voorhis, largely by implying that Voorhis had Communist connections. His central charge was: "Voorhis has been endorsed by the PAC" (Political Action Committee, organized by the CIO). This was not only false, but Voorhis had a strong anti-Communist record as a member of the House Committee on Un-American Activities. He had introduced and seen passed unanimously the Voorhis Act, the only piece of legislation enacted by Congress that was opposed by both the Communist party and the German-American Bund.

Nixon continued his manipulation of the facts in his successful 1950 campaign for the Senate, against Helen Gahagan Douglas. A forceful anti-Communist, she had supported Harry Truman and had worked hard for the passage of bills providing military aid to free nations of Europe. "The Soviet Union," she wrote in *The New Republic,* August 29, 1949, "has done its utmost to prevent European recovery . . . has deliberately created an atmosphere of fear and danger." One of her champions at the time was Ronald Reagan, then a Democrat. Throughout the campaign, Nixon talked about nothing but Communism. He called Douglas the "pink lady," and issued a "pink sheet" on pink paper explaining her Communist connections. His false charges, official-seeming documents, fake committees, and phony polls convinced voters he had a noble cause.

His greatest single triumph of manipulation came on September 23, 1952, when he delivered his famous "Checkers speech" on national radio and television. In response to a disclosure that he had a secret fund provided by seventy-six wealthy Californians who had a special interest in his gaining power in Washington, he refuted the allegations of wrongdoing, not with evidence but with an impelling emotional appeal. He admitted that he had accepted a few gifts and said he was willing to return them all, except a little black-and-white cocker spaniel, Checkers, which had been a gift to his daughters. Checkers's picture was then shown on the TV screen. The total effect was a triumph. Darryl Zanuck called the speech "the most tremendous performance I have ever seen!"

In spite of his nickname Tricky Dick, his reputation for saying one thing and doing another, his failure in his 1960 campaign for President, his unsuccessful run for governor of California in 1962, and his being caught at deceptive practices in his earlier campaigns, he was still able to gain the presidency in 1968.

Even with the weight of evidence against him as he tried to cover up the biggest political scandal in American history, Watergate, he was still able to garner considerable support through protestations of superpatriotism and his need for secrecy in the interest of national security. In a radio address to the nation in February 1973, eight months after the Watergate break-in, President Nixon said he was asking Congress for laws requiring the death penalty for treason, sabotage, espionage, and other federal crimes. Of the draft evaders who had fled to Canada, he had said previously: "We cannot provide forgiveness for them. They must pay their price. The price is criminal penalty for disobeying the law of the land."

Only when the recorded evidence on the White House tapes showed his complicity and dishonesty did his manipulative persuasiveness fail to camouflage the facts effectively. He was revealed to be a victim of both the Peter Principle and the Nixon Principle,* proving that an ability that is an asset at the Slippery Gulch Rodeo can be effective at many levels but can become a liability when it reaches the highest office in the land.

Nixon Principle: If two wrongs don't make a right, try three.

4

Gloom at the Top

Whenever a man has cast a longing eye on offices, a rot-
tenness begins in his conduct.   —THOMAS JEFFERSON

The operation of the Peter Principle in politics and government
raises frequently asked questions about exceptions to the principle. What about individuals who are incompetent and through
study become competent? Is it possible for incompetents to be
promoted to levels on which they are competent? Why do some
incompetents get good ratings from their supervisors?

The serious hierarchiologist will not accept the easy explanation that the Peter Principle is not a law but a principle. It
really describes only a general trend or direction, not a hard-
and-fast rule. The statement that individuals *tend* to rise to their
levels of incompetence does not absolutely require an explanation for individuals who prefer to stay at their levels of competence. If it were not a principle but a law or rule, real exceptions
to it would have to be identified as such, and instances would
have to be explained. Because hierarchiology is a science and is
searching for the whole truth, we must explore even the apparent exceptions to the principle.

> COROLLARY 9: The Peter Principle, like evolution, shows no
> mercy.

APPARENT EXCEPTION NO. 1:
PERCUSSIVE SUBLIMATION

Individuals are promoted to their levels of incompetence; therefore a true promotion can only be a promotion *from* a position of competence. When an incompetent is promoted from a level of incompetence, he or she is receiving a pseudo-promotion.

> COROLLARY 10: Once an employee achieves a level of incompetence, inertia sets in and the employer settles for incompetence rather than dismiss the employee and look for a replacement.

The most direct solution to the problem of what to do with an incompetent is to move him or her out of the way. In olden times this was accomplished by firing. Changes in the law, the growth of professional organizations and unions, and the enforcement of seniority rules have caused a reduction in the use of this old-fashioned technique. But today, when an incompetent occupies a key position, getting him or her out of the way is still of utmost importance.

When Claude Hopper was promoted to his level of incompetence as department manager, he was in a key position to create havoc in his department as well as to be a bottleneck for the total organization. The competent chief executive, Hew Main, quickly perceived the situation and elevated Claude to vice-president, joining the seventeen others at that level. In other words, Hew kicked him upstairs or gave him a Percussive Sublimation. (To *sublimate* means to make a change in a socially acceptable manner, and *percussion* means bumping quickly.)

Percussive Sublimation served the organization in several ways.

1. It saved face because it covered the fact that Claude's previous promotion to manager was a mistake and instead made it appear to have been a smart move. Note how quickly Claude received another promotion.
2. It encouraged others to be competitive. If Claude could rise so fast, there was still hope for his fellow workers.
3. It moved Claude out of a critical job, for which he was unsuited, to an innocuous position.
4. It saved Claude from becoming an embittered malcontent at his level of incompetence and a danger to organizational morale. Demoting him would have been even worse. By being promoted, he suffered no indignity.
5. It maintained the hierarchy. As long as Claude and others were moving up and production was flowing, the hierarchy was working.
6. It separated the drones from the workers.

The higher an incompetent is in the pyramidal structure of an organization, the more of a bottleneck he or she becomes and the more urgent it is that he or she be Percussively Sublimated. Fortunately, in the business or corporate world, organizations are structured for this. There is no limit to the number of vice-presidents a corporation may have. When a president is incompetent, he can be appointed a director of the company or even be made chairman of the board.

Although Percussive Sublimation is a pseudo-promotion that moves an incompetent from a level of incompetence to a higher level, it is seldom resisted because the new position offers better pay and more status.

Unfortunately, the structure of the executive branch of our government lacks the advantages enjoyed in the private business sector. The founding fathers, for all their wisdom, failed to create an innocuous position for an incompetent President. To correct this, my first recommendation would be to make the presidency a lower-level job, by creating a new and higher position for a Premier General.

The creation of a higher-level office would increase the effectiveness of the office of the President. The Premier General would assume all the ceremonial functions that now occupy so much of the President's time. The President could then devote all his efforts to the role of head of government and to conducting the actual business of the country. The Premier General would be head of state and perform all the official ceremonial roles: entertaining dignitaries; bestowing gracious words of praise on civic groups, charitable organizations, and the winners of the Super Bowl; hosting state dinners; throwing out the first baseball; laying cornerstones; cutting ribbons; giving commencement speeches, and so forth. The United States would then have all the advantages of a limited monarchy with none of the disadvantages of an entrenched hereditary royal family. The practical benefits of a separate head of state and head of government are too far-reaching to be enumerated here, but any reasonable person can see the many advantages of having ceremonial functions uncorrupted by party politics and the temptations that the quest for power is heir to.

COROLLARY 11: Lust gets us into more trouble than sloth.

Several Presidents of the United States reached outstanding levels of incompetence. Ulysses S. Grant served two terms in the White House, from 1869 to 1877. A West Point graduate and career military officer, he was forced to resign his commission in 1854 because of heavy drinking. When the Civil War broke out, he was appointed colonel of a ragtag band of volunteers and, through his ability and political influence, rose rapidly to become commander of all the Union armies. Following the war he was elected President to fill an office that under his administration was plagued with corruption. Prominent Republicans were exposed for siphoning profits from the Union Pacific railroad. Government officials were involved in a whisky operation that defrauded the government of needed tax dollars, and his Secretary of War was impeached for taking bribes.

Lust gets us into more trouble than sloth.

Woodrow Wilson, former president of Princeton University, had a vigorous first term with an impressive legislative record. He was a most admired statesman, pacifist, and mastermind of the League of Nations. He only narrowly won reelection on the slogan "He kept us out of war." One month after his second inauguration, America was in World War I. In 1919 he suffered a paralytic stroke that significantly diminished his physical and mental energies. With Wilson unable to perform many of his duties, his wife, Edith Bolling Galt Wilson, commandeered the helm. For the remaining seventeen months of his presidency she, not too competently, ran the office of the President. Congress was outraged but unable to wrest the reins from her grasp.

Warren G. Harding, the twenty-ninth President, was elected in 1920 by 60.3 percent of the popular vote—the largest mandate then on record. His campaign slogan was "Return to normalcy." If, as skeptics suggest, corruption in government is normal, the Harding administration delivered on its promise.

Harding's largely unsupervised Cabinet was comprised of patronage appointees and unqualified friends. When his Secretary of the Interior leased government-owned oil reserves to business friends, the Teapot Dome scandal rocked the nation. By Harding's own admission, "I am not fit for this office and never should have been here."

President Richard M. Nixon did more to degrade American politics and destroy America's faith in itself than any other President. He lied and spied, berated the press, defied the courts, and repudiated Congress. If he had been elevated to Premier General when the Watergate scandal was exposed, the country would have been spared two years of agonizing over just how much he knew and just when he knew it, and the painful decision to institute impeachment proceedings would have been avoided.

Each of these Presidents was incompetent for a different reason, but each would have been a competent Premier General. Grant's drinking, Wilson's ill health, Harding's unfortunate business connections, and Nixon's dishonesty would not have impeded their carrying out the rituals of head of state. As a matter of fact, honesty and sobriety are often liabilities to social performance.

For example, Richard Nixon, whatever his flaws may have been, had the potential to become our greatest Premier General. The sense of pride he would have felt on receiving a promotion to this new and highest office of the land would certainly have caused his potential to blossom. He was the only President to visit all fifty states while in office. He opened up China and was well received in international circles. Not outwardly warm or easygoing, he presented an air of formality well suited to dignifying the social amenities of a nation. A devotee of regalia, Nixon proposed that the White House marine guard change to a braided and brassed uniform reminiscent of *The Student Prince*. His 1972 $4 million inaugural celebration, with its parades, concerts, receptions, and balls, was nothing short of a smash hit.

There need never be vacancies in the office of Premier General, as past Presidents could always be appointed to the post and several Premiers General at one time would be an asset.

> COROLLARY 12: There is a tendency for the person in the most powerful hierarchal position to spend all his or her time performing trivial tasks.

The office of the President has another major weakness that has been avoided in successful corporate structures. When a new president is required, a business empire has a pool of vice-presidents to choose from. If one is chosen for promotion who is not at his level of incompetence as vice-president, the odds that he will be a competent president are significantly enhanced. In government we are not so fortunate. When a President in office must be replaced because of his death, impeachment, or (one would hope) by Percussive Sublimation to Premier General, we are stuck with just one possible promotee.

If Woodrow Wilson had been appointed Premier General, Thomas Marshall would have been promoted to President. When asked about becoming President, he said that the thought depressed him. When asked what he would do if he became President, he replied, "I can't even think about it." Marshall never attended Cabinet meetings because, he said, if he couldn't have the $75,000 that went with the President's job, he wasn't going to do any of the work. He is best remembered for his profound observation: "What this country needs is a good five-cent cigar."

More than fifty years later, because of the corruption that drummed Spiro Agnew from office, we wound up with a President who hadn't even been elected Vice-President. Human fallibility being what it is, this country should have a group of Vice-Presidents. If a private corporation recognizes the need for twenty vice-presidents, should the country try to operate with only one?

APPARENT EXCEPTION NO. 2:
LATERAL ARABESQUE

When an incompetent occupies a key position, creating a bottleneck that impedes the function of an organization, the problem can be quickly resolved by moving him or her out of the road in either an upward direction (Percussive Sublimation) or sideways (Lateral Arabesque). Ideally, the Lateral Arabesque is accompanied by conferring upon the promotee a longer and more impressive title and moving him to a remote part of the building. In the case of government or a large corporation, this may mean a move to another office, region, or country. As long as this pseudo-promotion appears impressive to those outside the hierarchy, the move is successful; the hierarchy is preserved.

General William C. Westmoreland, commander of U.S. forces in Vietnam from 1964 to 1968, directed the battle at Khe Sanh and the American defense of Saigon during the Tet offensive. To the American public, the result was the realization that we were in a war we could not win. Westmoreland characterized this as "doom and gloom talk" and requested 206,000 more troops. That was too much. President Lyndon Johnson Lateral-Arabesqued Westmoreland back to Washington as Army Chief of Staff, effective June 1968, and appointed General Creighton W. Abrams commander of U.S. forces.

The benign nature of the Lateral Arabesque and Percussive Sublimation, and the agreeable results achieved by moving the promotee either up or sideways, make these the treatments of choice when firing is not feasible.

APPARENT EXCEPTION NO. 3:
HIERARCHAL EXFOLIATION

Gentle readers, no doubt you are asking why incompetents aren't fired. Sometimes, in extreme circumstances, they are, but the individuals at Akme Lead and Pewter Products, Inc., moved to their levels of incompetence and then stayed there because that hierarchy was designed to accommodate both the competents and the incompetents. As long as incompetence does not threaten the hierarchy, it is usually tolerated by the system. The reasons will become clear, but for now it is important to understand that hierarchies are established to maintain order and not to eliminate incompetence or to identify and reward competence. The usual goal in creating an organization is to get things done. But it must not be assumed that just because the organization is founded on good intentions it will therefore actually get good things done. Once the hierarchy is established, its own existence becomes its purpose. At Akme, Jerry Attrick muddles along as chief executive and the others keep their heads above water only because those beneath them have enough competence to keep them afloat.

COROLLARY 13: It's harder to get the job than to keep it.

Individuals may be selected on a basis of competence, for their entry-level jobs, but as they move up they tend to become arranged just as distribution theory would predict: the majority in the moderately competent group, with the competent and incompetent comprising the minorities, as illustrated in the graph.

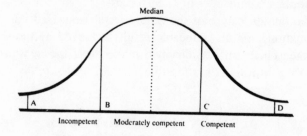

There are two rare types of individuals who do not fit into this structure: the supercompetent and the superincompetent. A supercompetent is usually someone who sees a better way of doing things. If Lou Cid, assistant office manager at Akme Lead and Pewter Products, Inc., designed a simple, efficient form to re-place the fourteen different forms used as internal requisitions, she would have upset Ann Jyna, who had designed most of the fourteen forms and had devised the elaborate system for filing them. Lou Cid could hardly expect to get approval for this in-novation from Ann Jyna. If she had introduced the new form without approval, she would have "exceeded her authority" and if she had taken her idea to Jerry Attrick, she would have been accused of "not following established guidelines" or "going over the head of her superior." Whichever of these behaviors she had chosen would have been cited at the time of her dismissal, along with statements such as "You don't seem to be happy here"; "You are a malcontent who doesn't fit into the way we do things at Akme"; "We are very proud of our Miss Jyna and find it difficult to understand why you don't want to follow the proce-dures she has established. You seem to be determined to upset our entire system." Supercompetence frequently leads to dis-missal because it disrupts the hierarchy. That is why it is more objectionable than impotence within an establishment. Ordinary incompetence is a bar to promotion, but is not a cause for firing.

The other way an establishment can protect itself from the disrupting influence of the supercompetents is through isolation. Mrs. Abel, a supercompetent first-grade teacher, could not be fired because she had tenure, did not exceed her authority, and was careful not to break the rules of her contract. By her place-ment in a remote area of the school and her exclusion from most staff and school activities, her threat to the establishment was minimized, although her effective teaching methods were still a threat to the orthodox way of doing things. Each year the prin-cipal had to cope with the complaints of grade-two teachers who reported that Mrs. Abel's pupils just didn't fit in, they had al-ready covered much of the second-grade work, and were pre-cocious about trying things that were beyond their grade level.

The other type of employee who threatens the hierarchy and therefore tends to get fired or isolated is the superincompetent.

When Jerry Attrick rose from Akme Lead Weight and Sinker to head Akme Lead and Pewter, he moved from being moderately competent to being incompetent. This did not disrupt the hierarchy, but if he had decided to make drastic changes in the company's product line that resulted in loss of the company's place in the market, he would have become a superincompetent and subject to firing. If Mal Larky's ethical incompetence had developed to a point where he was caught embezzling a large sum from company funds, he would have achieved superincompetence status. Employees in the two extreme classes, supercompetent and superincompetent, as shown in the completed graph, are alike subject to dismissal. This sloughing off of extremes is called Hierarchal Exfoliation.

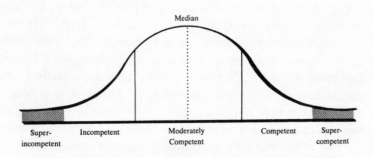

APPARENT EXCEPTION NO. 4:
FREE-FLOATING APEX

The sight of an administrator with nothing to administrate has puzzled observers who ask me: "How did he get there? There is no hierarchy beneath him to provide the ladder to his level." This strange situation can come about in two ways. Cutbacks are made starting at the base of the employment pyramid and the top administrators are the last to go. "Last hired, first fired" and other employment policies of hierarchies can eventually result in a pyramid consisting solely of the capstone suspended aloft without a base to support it. The Free-floating Apex can also occur when a department is moved to a different branch of the organization and the administrator is left behind with nothing to do.

APPARENT EXCEPTION NO. 5:
HIERARCHY HOPPING

Critics of the Peter Principle are fond of pointing out examples of individuals who have risen from incompetence to competence. According to them, Harry S Truman's failure in business and later success in politics is proof that the principle is invalid. Of course, they only prove their own incompetence by not reading the principle carefully. It states: "In a hierarchy . . ." Truman got out of the hierarchy where he failed into a hierarchy where he succeeded. Hierarchy Hopping explains why many early failures become successes.

Billy Bishop, regarded as the "worst cadet the Royal Military College ever had," became a Canadian hero in World War I as the ace fighter pilot who shot down a record number of enemy planes. Two previously unappreciated characteristics were responsible for his success: his exceptional eyesight and superb marksmanship. Owen Sound, Ontario, had been plagued with squirrels, and Bishop's father offered him 25 cents a squirrel. Billy Bishop's talent for shooting squirrels cost Will Bishop a small fortune. Billy could shoot ahead of a running squirrel and hit it every time. In France he had no wish to be taken prisoner, and he didn't like to take chances. As a fighter pilot those characteristics served him well. He spent as little time as possible in the dangerous pursuit of flying. He got within range of his target quickly, shot, and got out fast. His talent for killing was highly prized in the military, but there was not much opportunity for a successful career in that line of work in civilian life.

Ulysses S. Grant failed as a farmer and in business, yet in the military hierarchy in the Mexican War and the Civil War he

rose to outstanding success because he was a capable and skill-
ful military officer. Later, when he was promoted to another hierarchy, he chose associates who gave even dirty politics a bad
name.

APPARENT EXCEPTION NO. 6: PROMOTEE AND ASSIGNMENT ADAPTATION

Occasionally a promotee enters a new hierarchal level and at
first is confused or lacks confidence. He may have the aptitude
for the work but lack specific experience, knowledge, or skill
for the task at hand. With time, experience, or training he becomes competent. In other words, at first he appears to be a victim of the Peter Principle but later proves not to be. This should
be a warning to avoid haste in judging the competence of new
appointees. Allow some time for adaptation to the new position
before determining if the promotee is at his level of incompetence. If the aptitude is there, education and time will help. If
the appointee lacks aptitude for the job, nothing can help.

There are those who believe an individual can be successful
at anything if he tries hard enough, but my observations do not
support this concept. Back at Akme, Cal Luss, competent at
dealing with metals, was having great difficulty in his personal
relationships. The more he tried to work with people the worse
things seemed to get. Jerry Attrick had so many complaints that
he surrounded Cal with assistants competent in personal relations, and they dealt directly with the staff. Things were going
so well in the metals department that everyone remarked on how
well Cal Luss had grown into the job. In reality the job had been
cut back to fit Cal's limitations. Assignment Adaptation has been
responsible for many success stories where the individual is
credited with "learning the ropes."

Winston Churchill fared badly in politics in the 1930's but
went on to success in the war years. He had not changed; the
job had changed. Politics in wartime and politics in peacetime

are significantly different. He was a poor follower but a strong leader. He lacked the patience and finesse required in democratic peacetime politics, but when the job changed, requiring a leader to rally a nation to battle, he was ready and able. He had not climbed from failure to success. The assignment changed and then he was a success.

APPARENT EXCEPTION NO. 7: PATERNAL IN-STEP

In the old fashioned family business it was an accepted custom for the father to bring his sons into the firm with the conviction that the eldest son would eventually "step into the old man's shoes." Preferential treatment of the sons was accepted as a privilege of company ownership—the Paternal In-Step. The accelerated upward movement of the son destined to fill his father's shoes often brought the heir apparent to his level of incompetence at an earlier age than would ordinarily have been the case. Concerned with keeping the business in the family, the father was determined that his son would wear the shoes even if he couldn't fill them.

In today's bureaucracies the paternal role has been taken over by big brother. Government agencies are staffed by civil servants placed in slots or rigidly specified positions. The budget of the agency depends on each slot being filled; therefore slot-filling is essential. Whether the job needs doing, or the slot occupant can do it, is of secondary importance.

The important thing to realize in the Parental In-Step or civil-servant-for-every-slot situation is that the shoe wearer and slot occupant are put there to occupy a certain space in the organization, and to expect more of them is unfair.

APPARENT EXCEPTION NO. 8: THE BROKEN RUNG

Critics of the Peter Principle are fond of pointing to examples of individuals who have become incompetent while staying on one level. While this does happen, a closer examination will reveal that it is not a violation of the principle.

The misunderstanding occurs because of our symbolic use of the ladder as the means of achieving success. The "ladder of success" is an apt analogy, but unfortunately we may overlook the fact that a real ladder, as well as "the ladder of success," can have a broken rung. The painter, competently painting a house, is rendered ineffective when the rung beneath his feet collapses. His situation is not unlike that of the competent Monterey sardine fisherman after the sardines were gone from the area—the rung upon which he was competent had disappeared.

In the horse and buggy days, the competent carriage builder, blacksmith, harness maker, wheelwright, and buggy-whip maker had respected and financially secure positions in the economic order of things. The mass production and popularity of automobiles changed all that. Members of those honored trades, neither through climbing nor through loss of their skills but simply through staying at what they could do well, found themselves unemployable. The rung they had climbed to, and on which they had felt confident and competent, had given way.

Similarly, many jobs are changing because of advances in technology, and a highly competent occupant on any rung of the ladder may become obsolete through failure to move with the times or to change position quickly enough when that rung shows the first signs of collapse.

Individuals who climb to what seems to be a secure level of competence and stolidly remain there, unresponsive to changing conditions, may become victims of delayed incompetence because their former competence level no longer exists.

> It is the nature of a man as he grows older to protest
> against change, particularly change for the better.
> —JOHN STEINBECK

Many jobs are changing because of advances in technology.

APPARENT EXCEPTION NO. 9:
SEXUAL DISCRIMINATION

The Peter Principle is an Equal Opportunity Employer. Why then have I written mainly about men who have risen to their levels of incompetence in high office? Because until recently, prejudice, both legal and social, has limited the opportunities for women to enter certain professions and to achieve high office. Today, although many of the legal obstacles have been removed, traditional ideas about man as the leader endure.

> A woman has to be twice as good as a man to go half as far.   —FANNIE HURST

Laws and social barriers protected some women from rising to their levels of incompetence while, at the same time, they prevented others from developing their abilities and participating fully in all aspects of society. As these prejudicial barriers have been lowered, we have seen an increase in the numbers of women ascending to successful leadership positions in the professions, government, and industry.

> PETER'S SEXIST PRINCIPLE: Most hierarchies were established by men who monopolized the upper levels, thus depriving women of their rightful share of opportunities to achieve their own levels of incompetence.

For women to achieve their potential it is essential that they not be protected from that potential, whether for competence or incompetence.

> No person should be denied equal rights because of the shape of her skin.   —PAT PAULSEN

Although men have a long history of climbing to incompetence, there have been some small clues, in the performance of roles shared by men and women—such as talk show host, celebrity, and actor—that women have a similar potential for making mistakes. Back in the 1950's, when Virginia Graham hosted a talk show on NBC, she and Angie Dickinson were discussing motherhood. Virginia asked Angie about her daughter: "How old was she when she was born?"

The celebrated and talented American dancer Isadora Duncan had a long, flowing scarf around her neck when she went for a ride in an open car. The scarf became entangled in a rear wheel and it broke her neck, causing her death.

Myrna Loy was offered the lead in *It Happened One Night,* Frank Capra's film masterpiece. She thought the film would be unsuccessful because much of the action took place on a bus, so she turned it down. It was one of the biggest successes in the history of movies. Claudette Colbert played the part and won an Academy Award.

For counterproductive action on the part of a women's group, first prize goes to an organization in Ortow, England. The men of the town had barred the women from the local pub. The women fought back. They announced that in protest against the exclusion, they would boycott the pub.

Political competence is most difficult to evaluate objectively because of the overriding influence of partisan politics, but if the purpose of the Environmental Protection Agency is to protect the environment, Anne Gorsuch Burford was objectively incompetent on many counts. As head of the EPA, she set up her office two miles from EPA headquarters in room 6124 of the Interior Department. Burford reorganized the EPA and eliminated the enforcement division. She announced her support for doubling the allowable pollution rate for automobiles. EPA's regional offices were rendered practically useless, as all decisions had to go to Washington for approval and all but the smallest grants had to be okayed by Burford. Environmentally, she was a disaster. Politically, she aroused the wrath of both liberals and conservatives. Administratively, her department was in chaos. Bureaucratically, she failed on all counts to protect her department; her leader, James Watt; her backer, Joseph Coors, brewer and conservative supporter who had recommended her for the job; and she even failed to protect herself and her position.

> The President doesn't want any yesmen and yes-women around him. When he says no, we all say no.
> —ELIZABETH DOLE, assistant to President Reagan

Women have always had indirect power, through their influence on men and through their role in child rearing, although denied power in their own right. But even in the domestic sphere it is possible to rise to incompetence.

> The hand that rules the cradle rocks the world.
> —PETER DE VRIES

In a column in *The Washington Star,* Janet Kamnikar described how the role of a mother could change over time. "The other day, I had a revelation about the Peter Principle as it applied to me. I realized that getting a four-bedroom house had effectively promoted me to the level of my incompetence. Two children and our first small house I could handle—but that was no proof that I should be promoted."

She went on to describe a neighbor who had also become a motherhood victim of the principle, but in a different way. She had been a very competent and effective mother of babies, toddlers, and school-age children, but becoming the mother of a teenager had been her downfall.

COROLLARY 14: Equal opportunity means everyone will have a fair chance at becoming incompetent.

Women have always had indirect power through their influence on men.

APPARENT EXCEPTION NO. 10: PETER'S INVERT

A Peter's Invert is an employee preoccupied with input and unconcerned with output. In the normal course of events, we organize people and procedures in order to accomplish something—our activities are a means to an end. In bureaucracies there is a tendency for the personnel and procedures to become ends in themselves. In a productive organization an employee is valued for output—the number of widgets produced, orders filled, or customers served. In a bureaucracy it is more likely that an employee is valued for input—for supporting the rules and rituals, maintaining the status quo, and protecting the hierarchy.

Where input dominates, ritualistic behavior, conformity to established routines, proper deference to authority, and paperwork are most highly regarded.

"Moe doesn't make waves."

"Larry is steady and cooperative."

"Mo doesn't make waves."

"Curly is dependable."

What gets done is simply not as important as how well the organizational procedures are observed. This is an inversion of the ends-means relationship in which the paperwork itself is more important than the purpose for which it was intended. Taxpayers seeking information, patients trying to get medical help, customers wanting service, when they come up against a Peter's Invert are convinced they have encountered an obstinate, unfeeling incompetent. But from within the bureaucracy, the Invert may be highly valued for his or her contribution to the smooth operation of the hierarchy. The Invert doesn't make waves, never breaks rules, tolerates no deviations in procedures even in emergency situations, and, above all, consistently supports the internal structure of the organization.

The Invert views outsiders not as a public to be served but

as the source of information to serve the bureaucracy's forms, rituals, procedures, and data banks. The citizen's simple inquiry is met with: "Yes, but I'm not allowed to give out that information"; "I have no opinion. After you file your applicaton, we will consider your request"; "If you will wait in that line the information officer will tell you which line to wait in."

THE SHIP OF STATE

We have seen that the apparent exceptions to the Peter Principle are in fact only manifestations of the principle in action. Not only do individuals rise to levels of incompetence; whole departments may become ineffective. The following examples help to illustrate how incompetence manifests itself in government service.

> It is hard to feel individually responsible with respect to the invisible processes of a huge and distant government.   —JOHN GARDNER

The Veterans Administration Medical Center in Long Beach issued a memo to employees: If they received any phone threats against the President, they should make a note of the "name and Social Security number of the caller, if given."

The U.S. Park Service decided to install toilets for backpackers on the Appalachian Trail. One toilet, five miles from the highway on a mountaintop, had to be equipped with wheelchair ramps to conform to government regulations.

A story from the Associated Press reports that in India, Pratap Singh Daulta has been the minister for fisheries and forests of Hariana State for the past three months, although, he says, the state has no fish and no forests.

The Small Business Administration established a committee to distribute bonuses to the most effective managers in the agency. The nine-member review board, comprised of the agency's top executives, considered carefully. When the bonuses were awarded, seven of the nine panel members were on the list. One of the seven was even awarded a bonus of $4,760 for initiating the bonus system.

The governor of Massachusetts agreed to give his state's highways a "safety upgrade," though not because the highways were unsafe. Governor Michael Dukakis was told by federal officials that the upgrade was a condition of a $50 million grant to the state. The same officials warned Dukakis that if he didn't spend the entire $50 million in one year, he would not get a grant the following year.

Buses on the Hanley-to-Bagnall run in Staffordshire, England, regularly failed to stop for passengers. In response to complaints, Councillor Arthur Cholerton explained that if buses stopped to pick up passengers, the timetable would be disrupted.

A rural California resident had not received any mail for several days. He inquired at the local post office and was informed by his carrier that recent rains had caused a rut near his mailbox. Since she could not pull close enough to deliver the mail, she simply withheld it. The man asked why he hadn't been notified. "I did notify you. There's the notice right there!" she insisted. The carrier pointed to the official notice, which was right on top of the mail she hadn't delivered.

When Dr. John Ziegler of Cincinnati sent for a federal government publication called "Handbook for Emergencies," he carefully jotted down the number of the publication, #15,700. Two weeks later 15,700 copies of the booklet arrived at his residence.

Social Security Commissioner John Svahn called it "astounding." A number of dead people have received monthly Social Security checks from the Department of Health and Human Services, some for as long as fifteen years. In a cross-check of Social Security recipients with Medicare reports listing the deceased, 8,518 cases of friends and relatives cashing benefit checks were revealed. Another review of 1,290 cases showed that 190 were actually alive but were reported as deceased. Removing the dead from the Social Security rolls will save $26 million the first year.

Bob Green, a left-handed postal worker in Seattle, was told he must sort the mail with his right hand or be fired. When a group of postal managers inspected the post office where Green worked, they told his supervisors he should work right-handed because "the postal manual says letters will be held in the left hand and distributed with the right hand." Green told his supervisor, Ed Scott, that he had been left-handed for forty-four years and using his right hand would cut down his productivity. Scott told him he must abide by the rule.

Green did, and his speed was reduced by 50 percent. The American Postal Workers Union was looking into the situation. They estimated it would take the government three months to sort it out.

The Associated Press reported that a nuclear power plant in Knoxville, Tennessee, was closed for seventeen days because an employee's protective boot fell into Unit 1 of the three-reactor Browns Ferry Nuclear Plant. The seven-state Tennessee Valley Authority and federal nuclear officials eventually figured out a way to be certain the galosh had disintegrated before resuming operation of the generator. The shutdown cost $2.8 million. The TVA pointed out afterward that the shutdown wouldn't have occurred if the galosh had stayed on the worker's foot.

Following the recent publication of a new edition of Samuel Pepys's *Diary,* its British publisher received a government notice asking whether the author was receiving a state pension, and whether he had declared his current income. Pepys died in 1703.

Canadian government flight regulations prohibit persons from "entering an aircraft in flight."

Hugh Cameron, business manager of a Southern California high school district, used a courier to deliver paychecks, directives, and correspondence around his district because it was quicker, more efficient, and thousands of dollars cheaper than the normal mail service. At the end of a seven-year battle, the Postal Service ruled that the materials transported by couriers were letters, and "as such, are being illegally transported to avoid payment of postage." They informed him that because this was state work, he could continue to use couriers only if he also affixed postage and had someone cancel the postage.

The Department of Agriculture funded a $113,417 study and found that mothers prefer children's clothing that doesn't require ironing.

Attorney Stan Kelton has a number that is different by one digit from that of the Los Angeles County switchboard. One day a man identifying himself as a road-department worker phoned wanting to know why his paycheck had been docked for taking a sick day when he still had two sick days coming. An irritated Kelton told him, "The reason you were docked was that we happened to know you weren't sick at all. You were drinking in a bar all day." The county employee responded, "Uh, well, okay. Thank you very much. Goodbye."

The City of Washington, D.C., has warehoused enough Styrofoam balls to last for 40 years, enough modeling clay to last 15 years, enough red oil paint and cotton swabs to last 100 years, and a 561-year supply of light bulbs. Also on hand, the city has 2,100 new snow shovels purchased in 1962 and never used.

> Nothing is easier than spending public money. It does not appear to belong to anybody. The temptation is overwhelming to bestow it on somebody.
> —CALVIN COOLIDGE

5

Business as Usual

Peter's Business Principle: If you do something wrong you're
fined; if you do something right you're taxed.

Even when they are presiding over turmoil and disorder, corporate executives still believe that they are competent, efficient,
dynamic leaders and manipulators of men and women. The high
regard in which business executives are held by many otherwise
rational citizens indicates that, to a large extent, executives successfully foist these myths on the general public.

The following case studies are presented not in praise or in
condemnation of the executives involved. They are simply stories of individual bureaucratic organizations and the executives
who operated them. They are neither tales of the Great American Dream nor examples of the Great American Anti-Success
Myth, but simply an attempt to observe objectively, report reli-
ably, and comment rationally.

LATERAL ARABESQUE: INDUSTRIAL FILE NO. 207A

Most Americans who were around during the 1957–1959 Ford
Motor Company Edsel car debacle were aware of the major events
in the rise and fall of the Edsel. They witnessed the giant waves
of advertising and publicity that preceded the public launching

of the Edsel on September 4, 1957, or as the company called it, E-Day (Edsel Day). Two years later, Americans laughed at comedians' jokes about the Edsel as it sank from sight, leaving barely a ripple, although it will go down in history along with the *Titanic* as an example of the "perfect design" that failed.

In 1948, Henry Ford II proposed to the executive committee that studies be initiated regarding the feasibility of developing a revolutionary new car. Four years later, in 1952, the new-car project was under way with an energetic group called the Forward Products Planning Committee. In 1954 this committee submitted its six-volume report, indicating that increasing numbers of prosperous American citizens longed for a new, large, flashy, medium-priced car loaded with conveniences and gadgets. President Henry Ford II and the rest of the executives approved the Forward Products Planning Committee's report. A new agency to implement the report was established. It was called the Special Products Division and was headed by Richard Krafve. A young designer, Roy A. Brown, was put in charge of "styling" the new car. The idea was to design a car that would be unique in styling while at the same time familiar and popular.

The Edsel was advertised and promoted as the car with the features people wanted. Sure enough, public polls were conducted and suggestions were submitted for the name and other specifications of the car, but the name and design were arrived at without consulting the polls.

The task of naming the car was assigned to the Director of Planning for Market Research, who engaged the Columbia University Bureau of Research to conduct name-popularity polls in Peoria and San Bernardino. The research revealed that an automobile buyer who cares enough to vote is, like a man in love, incapable of anything resembling a rational decision regarding the object of his infatuation.

Although science had failed in this instance, the problem was resolved when Krafve suggested to members of the Ford family that the new car be called the Edsel in memory of Edsel Ford, the only son of Henry Ford, founder of the company.

The styling was not achieved with bold strokes of a designer's pen, but rather emerged from more than four thousand executive decisions about the shape of a door handle, the line of a fender, the amount of chrome, and so forth. Krafve and the Special Products Division reasoned that if they made the right decision on each of four-thousand-plus occasions, they would eventually produce the stylistically perfect car. By 1955, Roy A. Brown, with the help of Richard Krafve and the Special Products Division, had the Edsel completely styled. Its eye-catching feature was a novel, toilet-seat-shaped radiator grill, positioned vertically in the center of a conventional wide front end. They had achieved their objective of a blend of the unique and the familiar. The rear-end design was also unique. It consisted of widespread horizontal wings, the likes of which had never been seen on automobiles before the Edsel. The interior's unique contribution to easy living was a cluster of automatic-transmission push buttons on the hub of the steering wheel.

In the spring of 1957, Edsels were rolling off the assembly line. The publicity campaign kept public interest and curiosity at concert pitch. On E-Day the public was treated to its first view of the Edsel. Unfortunately, the car never caught the public fancy. So few were purchased that the company lost more than $3,000 on each one sold. The total amount of the company's loss has not been revealed, but it is probably in excess of $350 million.

The early Edsels were plagued with imperfections. The push buttons tended to stick, hoods and trunks would not open, and oil leaks appeared shortly after delivery. Krafve explained that all new-model cars have bugs in them. David Wallace, the market researcher, pinned the Edsel disaster on the Soviet *sputnik*, which, he claimed, shattered the myth of American technical superiority. Roy A. Brown, the designer, blamed the fiasco on bad timing and claimed that styling of the automobile had little or nothing to do with its failure. Apparently the executives were blameless and the Edsel just happened to be the wrong car for the wrong market at the wrong time.

The Edsel made United States business history by setting a

new record: the Edsel multimillion-dollar Ford Motor Company write-off. This provides an ideal illustration of the way in which the entire divisional management of a giant corporation can rise to its level of incompetence. But, more importantly, it shows how the individual managers of such a fiasco can be retained through sideways promotion. Most of those responsible for the Edsel stayed on and relocated within the company. For example, Roy A. Brown went on to become Ford's chief stylist of commercial vehicles. Richard Krafve became assistant to Robert S. McNamara, at that time a divisional vice-president at Ford Motors.

PETER'S TENURE PRINCIPLE: A man is known by the company that keeps him.

HIERARCHAL EXFOLIATION FILE NO. 7

Originally, the C5A military aircraft was conceived by the Pentagon as a monstrous cargo plane. It was to have 1,700 square feet of usable level floor space, with an airlift capacity of more than 200 tons. The inevitable committee or planning group was assembled. The Lockheed Aircraft Corporation contracted to build the planes at $28.5 million each. The planning group then established liaison with a vast number of departments within the military complex. The plane-planning group coordinated all the accumulated data and integrated everybody's ideas into the plans for the C5A. The original monster became a lumbering mammoth that included additional specifications to meet the demands of all the participants. The additional weight required increased takeoff and landing capabilities, so specifications and costs spiraled upward. The result was a $29 million overrun per plane—double the contract price.

Ernest Fitzgerald, an air force auditing officer, noticed that expenses were far outrunning estimates. He began asking questions. Lockheed and the Pentagon were not amused. Fitzgerald was first transferred, then isolated in an obscure position, and then fired. The air force's explanation for firing Fitzgerald was ironically described as "to save expenses."

As an auditing officer, Ernest Fitzgerald's responsibility was to identify where government expenditures were going. He did his job so well that he got fired, thereby becoming a Supercompetent Exfoliate.

> PETER'S COMPETENCE PRINCIPLE: The way to avoid mistakes is to gain experience. The way to gain experience is to make mistakes.

FREE-FLOATING APEX FILE NO. 11

At RCA, David Sarnoff made huge profits and acquired great prestige from pioneering color television. His son, Robert Sarnoff, was hard put to top this achievement but tried it in the computer field. The RCA Computer Division had a good reputation in the industry but was still a dwarf beside the IBM giant. In 1969, L. Edwin Donegan was recruited by RCA from IBM Data Processing Division sales department. Donegan's star rose quickly at the RCA Computer Division. By 1971 he was head of a new organization within the company, RCA Computer Systems, as well as corporation vice-president and general manager. He surrounded himself with IBM men and fired the RCA old guard or relegated them to nonperson status.

RCA made the greatest investment in its history in the computer division. Donegan and his recruits from IBM tried a variety of tactics to capture the IBM market, but every strategy failed. Robert Sarnoff eventually canceled the general-purpose computer program, and RCA got a $490 million tax write-off, beating the old record of the Ford Motor Company Edsel write-off and setting a new high as a business flop.

L. Edwin Donegan is no longer director of a ten-thousand man organization, but he is still in charge of the division and a near-empty building. Most of his former supporters are gone. They had hitched their wagon to a falling star.

Donegan had climbed to the top and stayed there even though it was the top of an empty administrative structure. He had become a Free-floating Apex.

PETER'S LEVITATION PRINCIPLE: When the foundation of a pyramid erodes, the top can still be supported on nothing but money.

IN SEARCH OF COMPETENCE

Of course these true stories support the Peter Principle, but they are of real value only if we can derive some new insights from them. Not all individuals are eligible for promotion. Some are not promoted because they are thought to be indispensable where they are; thus they have risen to their levels of indispensability. When an individual's level of incompetence and indispensability coincide, we have that strange anomaly the Indispensable Incompetent. An inept employee who has strong union support is an Indispensable Incompetent and his department head is between a rock and a hard place. A company with a leader who has risen to a level of managerial incompetence, but who has a fine public image and has just received a good-citizenship award, has an Indispensable Incompetent on its hands. If it gets rid of him, it is in big trouble. If it keeps him, it is in big trouble.

It is fair to conclude from the above cases that losing $490 million need not be a hindrance to executive survival, while attempts to save millions may get you fired.

PETER'S EVALUATION PRINCIPLE: Either superincompetence or supercompetence may be offensive to the establishment.

We also have seen that great success in manufacturing automobiles or television sets or widgets does not bestow wisdom in the selection of new projects or products.

PETER'S INVESTMENT PRINCIPLE: Fools rush in where wise men fear to trade.

Another observation one can make is that executive survival is unrelated to professional competence. As a matter of fact, some of the most entrenched management survivors have a pathological inability to function competently.

PETER'S EXPECTATION PRINCIPLE: What happens is not only stranger than we imagine, it is stranger than we *can* imagine.

Business has so many facets that its areas of potential incompetence seem unlimited. This is why the following examples only scratch the surface. On the other hand, we can only scratch the surface, because when we scratch deeper we are beneath the surface.

General Motors equipped its cars with a shock-absorbing bumper, making a crash perfectly safe . . . at speeds up to 2.8 miles per hour.

A security guard in Los Angeles, Jose Yera, filed a suit against a manufacturer, Point Blank Armor. He claimed their bulletproof vest failed to protect him when he stabbed himself in the stomach to test the garment.

Security personnel at Pan Am were concerned about the number of miniature liquor bottles that were disappearing, so they rigged a clock device to the liquor cabinet to record the times of the thefts. In flight, a stewardess heard the ticking and thought there was a bomb aboard. The captain rerouted the plane to Berlin, where passengers were evacuated by the emergency exits. The unscheduled landing cost around $15,000. The little bottles of liquor cost 35 cents each.

The meat cutter at a hotel in Switzerland lost a finger and filed an insurance claim. The insurance company sent a claim investigator to the hotel. The claim investigator asked to work the machine. He lost a finger.

Sign in office: "The spare key to the First Aid Room is available in the First Aid Room."

Elizabeth Kovacs, a peanut packer at Q Peanuts Company in England, was fired for being consistently early for work. Her fellow workers complained to management, and management issued her a warning. When Ms. Kovacs didn't change her habit, she was fired. A company spokesman said, "We applaud our workers who arrive on time but that means on time and not too early."

Simmons & Company, the mattress manufacturer, launched a major sales campaign in Japan in 1963. Four years later they abandoned the plan as a total loss. The Japanese sleep on floor mats called futons.

The College of Engineering at the University of Hawaii spent nearly $9 million for a new building and equipment. When Holmes Hall was completed, $200,000 worth of the new equipment could not be used because the building lacked sufficient power outlets.

The curiosity of the new assistant manager of a Johannesburg, South Africa, hotel was piqued whenever he pushed the elevator button for the first floor, because he always arrived at the second floor. An investigation led to a locked door, which when opened revealed a first floor of fourteen rooms that had not been disturbed for twenty years or more. Some of the older staff members confessed that they remembered when the hotel once had a first floor.

A new solar-powered wristwatch is computer-programmed to tell the date and time for 125 years. The watch is guaranteed—for 2 years.

Long Island's Airborne Instrument Laboratory placed an ad for a process inspector in a local newspaper. When the ad appeared in the paper, a typographical error made it seem that the company wanted a "prouss" inspector. There is no such thing as a *prouss* in the electronics industry. The next morning a man called up for an interview. He claimed that he had two years' experience inspecting prousses.

Safeway Stores, Inc., was fined $50,000 in penalties and costs for selling cherry pies with no cherries. Though baked by Bell Best Pies, the pastries were sold under the store's own Ovenjoy label. Bell Best regularly used grapes as filler with the cherries, but when weather conditions pushed the price of cherries up, they eliminated them altogether.

Joseph Begley of Evesham, England, mailed two thousand cigarette coupons to the redemption center for a wristwatch. When no watch arrived, Begley wrote the company to ask why. He received three watches, so he sent back two. The next day, ten packages arrived from the cigarette company. The day after, he got eighteen. The third day, ten more came. He had amassed three tape recorders, a golf bag, a pressure cooker, two electric blankets, a cot, and a doll. When Begley asked the company to stop sending premiums, he got an apology and ten thousand coupons for his trouble. He took the coupons and ordered tools and a bedspread. He got two step ladders and a plant stand.

The office staff at Sunset House was having trouble using legal-size paper with the newly acquired Xerox machine. When the maintenance department was called, they discovered that an error had been made in this new machine, despite millions spent in research and design. Standard legal size is 8½″ by 14″. In the new copier, legal paper had to be trimmed to fit—to 8½″ by 13″.

The *National Underwriter* magazine reported that the computer of an automobile insurance company sent bills for $0.00 to a St. Louis client. The man called his agent when the computer sent a "final notice" threatening cancellation. The agent decided the best course was to send the computer a check for $0.00. When the insured did, he received a thank-you note saying that his policy would be continued.

Penn Country Farms of New Holland, Pennsylvania, prepares frozen fried chicken for supermarket sales. When their fried chicken breasts did not fit in the normal package, it was discovered that the breasts had been cut in half the wrong way. Fifty-eight thousand pounds of breasts had been cut that way before the error was caught.

After ninety years of construction, the cathedral in Corcuetos, Spain, collapsed the day following its completion in 1625.

Sign in a restaurant: "Customers who consider our waitresses uncivil should see the manager."

At the Howard Hotel in Baltimore, contractors lit fires in the boilers, then noticed they had forgotten to install the chimney.

General Telephone Company in Los Angeles was making a film for its employees. The script included this dramatized scene, showing how to handle customer complaints with humor.

CUSTOMER: You just can't rely on that damn phone company for anything, can you?

EMPLOYEE: You get your bill every month, don't you?

A company source said the scene was excised from the film.

Contractors in Mozambique were building an addition to a seven-year-old hospital. They made a hole in a wall and found about $125,000 worth of equipment and a forgotten maternity ward. Hospital officials believed someone had put up a wall instead of a door.

A number of space toys, like the Battlestar Galactica, are so designed that if a child puts the front end of the spaceship in his mouth, a projectile is released with sufficient force to drive it down the child's windpipe. This is obviously a misuse of the toy because it was not intended to be used by children under three years of age. Following serious injuries to several small children, the manufacturer resolved the problem by placing a notice on the outside of the box warning children not to use it this way.

From a package label: "This packet of ready-made pastry will make enough for four persons or twelve tarts."

A new all-glass building in Arlington, Virginia, had its twenty-four lavatories equipped with frosted glass, which seemed to afford perfect privacy, but in due course a passerby perceived that from outdoors there was an unimpeded view of proceedings within. The one-way glass had been installed backward. When informed of this, an executive hurried out, took one look, and turned crimson. "My God! That's my secretary!" he cried.

Archie R. McCardell was chairman of the ailing International Harvester for two and a half years. During that time, he was paid $1.4 million per year even though the company lost $397 million in 1980 and $393 million in 1981.

Only days after General Motors had negotiated with the United Auto Workers for wage cuts, the company voted to restore bonuses to its top six thousand executives. The union's outrage forced GM to abandon its plan.

It may be a commentary on the times that page A-7 of the central Los Angeles telephone directory was headed "Survival Guide" but was otherwise a blank page.

Business will be better or worse.
—CALVIN COOLIDGE

6

To Whom It May Concern

There is no greater lie than the truth misunderstood.
—WILLIAM JAMES

A zoologist, studying the hyena, maintains objectivity about the hyena's behavior, although he may feel compassion for its victims. The hierarchiologist studying human behavior must have a similarly scientific approach. Although we are aware of disastrous things going on because of the Peter Principle, the reason for our study is not moralistic but scientific. It is not enough that we study the undesirable outcomes of excessive escalation; we should also examine the reasons we climb to our levels of incompetence.

If you are not one up, you're one down.
—STEPHEN POTTER

The undesirability of persons remaining at their ultimate levels is more than just their contribution of incompetence to a world already oversupplied; if individuals stay too long at their levels of incompetence, they erode the structure of the organization. Their presence demonstrates to others that competence is not a requirement for success. It also explains why it doesn't matter whether a bureaucracy expands or contracts; overhead grows at a constant rate.

102

While the Peter Principle accurately describes human behavior, it does not provide an answer to the question "Why do human beings climb to their levels of incompetence?" The most popular answer is: "It's natural to be aggressive and competitive." The irrefutable argument that human behavior is caused by human nature provides little real insight into either.

Abraham Maslow, the eminent psychologist, postulated that it was the nature of human beings to struggle onward and upward because when one group of needs is satisfied, a higher level of needs presents itself. Several different needs exist within each individual, and these needs relate to each other in the form of a hierarchy. Once essential physiological survival needs are satisfied, safety needs become dominant; then social needs, esteem or ego needs, and finally self-actualization needs. The social needs are concerned with establishing one's position relative to others. Ego needs include recognition and prestige, confidence and leadership, success and competence. Maslow's concept is one of the most attractive of all the theories that propose human nature as an explanation for our struggle ever upward.

Human aggressiveness is expressed in many ways, from the subtle quest for social approval to acts of violence committed in the attempt to gain physical dominance. In some situations we try to get ahead of others on the job, on the golf course, in debate, or in a gain of status. At other times, ascendence over others results in increased income, bonuses, prizes, and rewards. Symbolic battles are fought using a rigid set of rules on the chessboard and the football field, and fights to achieve symbolic death are performed in fencing, wrestling, and boxing. Competition without rules can lead to individuals engaging in hand-to-hand combat and to nations engaging in war. The evidence is clear that the human species has a great capacity for aggressiveness, whether played out symbolically, channeled into organized competition, or expressed in acts of violence.

On the other hand, even in our modern, violent society, many individuals are unaggressive and nonviolent, and a few rather remote tribes are still uncompetitive. Traditionally, the nomadic

Human aggressiveness is expressed in many ways.

Eskimos of the American Arctic cooperatively shared food and shelter among the members of the clan and settled disputes without resorting to violence. The Tangu people of New Guinea shared food equally among tribal members and engaged in games in which the object was to end in a draw. The Semai farmers of Malaya avoid violence of every kind. Historically, many nomadic tribes that survived by hunting or gathering natural vegetation were not competitive with one another, nor were they defensive of territory. Although the world was eventually dominated by the more aggressive, competitive, and territorial peoples, the existence of tribes and individuals who were not and are not aggressive and competitive leads us to question the belief that these characteristics are a part of human nature. At least we cannot accept, on the evidence, that aggressiveness and competiveness are universal or essential aspects of human nature.

> We savor power not when we move mountains and
> tell rivers whither to flow, but when we can turn men

into objects, robots, puppets, automata or veritable animals. Power is power to dehumanize.

—ERIC HOFFER

Up until recently, neurologists viewed the human brain as a gray, soggy computer divided into two equal halves, the left and right hemispheres. Then research discovered that the hemispheres have unique functions: The left brain manages language functions while the right brain handles spatial-perceptual matters. The left brain does a kind of linear, analytical, deductive thinking, and the right brain sees the big picture and engages in a kind of integrative, creative thinking.

When there is a fairly even balance in the strength of the two hemispheres, the individual can function logically, organize step-by-step procedures, write coherent instructions, and do all the left-brain things, while the right brain is able to take the overview necessary to understand the meaning of the left-brain details and their relationships to one another. When an individual has one hemisphere that is much more powerful than the other, he or she uses that hemisphere for most problem solving, whether it is appropriate or not. The right-brain dominant person with a weak left, when confronted with a problem requiring detail analysis, will either deal in broad generalization or ignore the data and jump to conclusions impulsively. Individuals with a dominant left brain and a weak right brain will deal in detail and analysis, compulsively making rules and regulations but never seeing the whole picture. They are so immersed in process, they never see or understand the meaning of their activity in a larger context.

It is the left-brain dominated individual who mindlessly climbs the Peter Principle ladder, who tends to be authoritarian, and who ultimately makes the rules and sets the standards for society. Left-brain domination explains why, within bureaucracies and other rigid hierarchies, some individuals are much more prone to the methodical, compartmentalized, ritualistic kinds of behavior for which bureaucrats are so famous.

> More humbly but not less ardently, if still on the lower
> rungs of the ladder, comes the Lifeman, pursuing each
> petty ploy till he, too, has achieved this state of One
> Upness. —Stephen Potter

There is one conclusive fact to be gained from the study of psychology. The behavior that produces a feeling of satisfaction, that is followed by a feeling of satisfaction, is the behavior that tends to be repeated. From our first days, the gratification of our physical needs for food and warmth along with the satisfaction of our emotional needs for security are reinforcers of our behavior. When a baby smiles or makes speechlike sounds, it is more likely to be hugged, patted, stroked, or talked to, and these responses produce feelings of satisfaction in the baby. As the infant learns to walk, talk, feed itself, and become toilet-trained, it gains parental approval that reinforces these accomplishments. When the child goes to school, achievement of good grades and athletic success are rewarded with recognition and praise from parents, teachers, and peers, along with such other rewards as prizes, money, ribbons, and certificates. If the young person stays in school and successfully climbs the educational hierarchy, he or she acquires social status and is awarded academic degrees and/or professional certification.

Upon entering the world of work, the individual places his foot on a lower rung of another ladder in which each step up is rewarded with a raise in pay and an increase in status.

In our lives, each step up the developmental stairs, the educational hierarchy, and the career ladder is rewarded. Climbing behavior is consistently reinforced and becomes firmly established. It is a conditioned response.

> The most beautiful as well as the most ugly inclina-
> tions of man are not part of a fixed, biologically given
> human nature but result from the social process.
> —Erich Fromm

The behavior that produces a feeling of satisfaction tends to be respected.

We are members of a strange species that devotes its energies to climbing the ladder of success in order to make money to buy things we don't need to impress people we don't like. It may be an aspect of the nature of humans to climb compulsively in spite of the lack of a rational reason. It could be a manifestation of a neurological imbalance in which the left brain so dominates behavior that climbing the hierarchal ladder is the only way out of present dilemmas that is available to those afflicted with this abnormality. My studies have shown nearly all bureaucrats and many administrators are so left-hemisphere dominated that they are incapable of doing anything more constructive than a linear kind of thinking. Certainly it is the left-brain individual who is neurologically best equipped to organize his or her step-by-step ascent of the hierarchy. And, of course, all of us are reinforced in our climbing behavior so that it becomes a conditioned response to move up the organization as far as time and opportunity will let us go.

It is highly probable that all three of these unconscious forces are powerful influences, but we are rationalizers and try to give conscious reasons for our behavior. We try to justify why, when we have all the money or income required to meet our real needs, we still try to get more. We complain about our burden of responsibility and yet strive for higher rank and greater responsibility. When we can perform our assigned tasks competently while avoiding undue stress, we say the job lacks challenge and request promotion to a level of worry, frustration, and possible incompetence. Many may feel that such irrational behavior requires a rational explanation.

We have attained a high material standard of living and possess most things in abundance. We spend a bundle on entertainment and invest fortunes on health, beauty, and reducing aids. Our medical costs are astronomical. One would expect that with all this we would be happy, healthy, and satisfied.

> Considering the precarious conditions under which the greater part of the human race had previously lived, the miserable dearth and scarcity and near-starvation, the besetting anxiety of trying to make both ends meet, one can well understand this new preoccupation with quantity.   —LEWIS MUMFORD

We believe that if a little is good, then more is better. Yet, if you've got one watch you know what time it is and if you've got two, you're never quite sure. We believe that we can escape from problems, frustrations, and feelings of futility through promotion or escalation to a higher position. But a promotion may mean only that we take orders from a better class of people. We believe that more is better and up is better. We believe that with more authority we would get more accomplished. We believe that more possessions, a bigger house or a second home, another car or another television set or a sailboat or a yacht will improve our lives. We believe that money and status will give us the good life. We believe that rising to our level of incompetence is fulfillment. We believe we should work and worry

We believe that if a little is good, then more is better.

and climb the success ladder. How else can one finance a heart attack?

> Ring around the roses,
> Coronary thrombosis,
> Seizure, seizure,
> All fall down.
> —A. BARD

This belief system is as old as Lucifer and the fall of the angels. Consider the dream of Jacob's ladder:

> And he dreamed, and behold a ladder set up on the earth, and the top of it reached to heaven: and behold the angels of God ascending and descending on it.
> —Genesis 28:12

The deterioration of the class system was followed by a new hierarchy of status based on money.

We believe that money and status will give us the good life.

> To succeed in the world, we do everything we can
> to appear successful.   —LA ROCHEFOUCAULD

Material wealth had the advantage of being unidimensional. Quantity was the sole requirement, so that one need only have more than someone else to have greater status. When our ancestors were establishing the social order in the New World, money not only became the simplest and easiest measure of status, but also offered the citizenry both opportunity and incentive to enter the system and gain status.

> The American doctrine of materialism was a force for
> individual and national strength.

> In America, as long as competition for material re-
> wards was keen and ambition to achieve these re-
> wards was strong, what resulted was not weakness

through self-indulgence but power through productivity.

American wealth began with personal austerity and self-denial.
—RICHARD M. HUBER, *The American Idea of Success*

Profit is a matter of numbers of dollars. Everybody knows what a dollar is and everybody agrees that it is a Good Thing. Its great charm is that it can be counted. It is definite. It is simple. Everybody understands and appreciates it. There is no argument about it. The American loves the dollar because he is philosophically timid, more so, I think, than any human being who ever lived. He is not at home with anything he cannot count, because he is not sure of any other measure. He cannot estimate or appraise quality. This leaves him with quantity.
—ROBERT MAYNARD HUTCHINS

The new value system equates success with money, so that acquiring cash is both success and the symbol of success.

To moral flabbiness born of the exclusive worship of the bitch-goddess Success. That . . . with the squalid cash interpretation put on the word success . . . is our national disease.
—WILLIAM JAMES, to H. G. Wells, 1906

Those whose achievements could not be immediately evaluated in terms of cash value were placed low on the status hierarchy.

I told the story of the immigrant who failed because he refused to enter the American Milieu on its terms—to start accruing status on the basis of money.
—HARRY GOLDEN

Individuals, even at their levels of incompetence, still push on, attempting further escalation. One explanation for this behavior is the joy of accomplishment in one-upping or beating somebody.

> In all distresses of our friends,
> We first consult our private ends;
> While Nature, kindly bent to ease us,
> Points out some circumstance to please us.
> —Jonathan Swift

The one-up condition can be achieved in either of two ways. In a game the player who is better than all the rest can usually win but, occasionally, so can the individual who can interfere physically or psychologically with the play of his competitor. Most things being relative, success may result from your merit or others' failure.

> It's not enough that we should succeed,
> but our friends must fail as well.
> —La Rochefoucauld

When asked by his church rector for some investment advice, Jay Gould, the Wall Street tycoon and multimillionaire, made the pastor swear he would keep the advice secret; the pastor agreed. "Buy Missouri Pacific," said Gould. The clergyman did, and the stock went up for several months. Eventually the stock crumbled and the rector was wiped out. Sadly, he went to see Mr. Gould. "I took your advice and lost all my savings."

"I'm sorry," said Gould. "To restore your faith, I'm going to give you forty thousand for the thirty thousand you lost." Gould wrote out a check and the minister reluctantly accepted it.

"I must confess something," the minister said. "I didn't keep my word. I told several members of the congregation."

"Oh, I know that," came Gould's cheerful reply. "They were the ones I was after."

Impressing others has become such a preoccupation that the image and trappings of success are more valued than success itself.

> The vanity of being known to be trusted with a secret is generally one of the chief motives to disclose it. —SAMUEL JOHNSON

Impressing others has become such a preoccupation that the image and trappings of success are more valued than success itself. The car one drives, where one lives, how one dresses, and the power one wields are more important to one's status than is his or her contribution to society. A growing army of experts offer advice on the success image, including what to wear, how to order food and wine, and how to choose the words you speak. The University of Chicago Graduate School of Business instructs students on selecting the proper wines when dining out with customers. *The New York Times* quoted an instructor: "While the lack of knowledge about choosing a proper wine may not kill a business deal, selecting the proper wine leaves a bit of room to impress the client." Other business schools now include wine selection as part of business administration.

> Americans are wasting a truly frightening amount of
> time either putting down others or living in a state of
> inner panic that others will put them down because
> they've used the wrong word, ordered the wrong wine,
> praised the wrong book, suggested the wrong restau-
> rant, or visited the wrong Greek island. The time
> wasted is time taken away from real communication
> with others, whether about individual human prob-
> lems or vital issues facing the nation and the world.
> Snobbery may be at its most dangerous when it
> counsels that one of those vital issues is chic and en-
> courages us to ignore others that are in fact of equal
> or greater importance.   —CHARLES PETERS

Early in our history we discovered how to communicate
through grunts and gestures, and it wasn't long before we began
to try to impress each other with the artistry of our expression.
As civilization advanced, the various hierarchal ranks within each
society could be identified not only by what they said but also
by their manner of speech. Social climbers attempted to adopt
the speech patterns, accent, and vocabulary of the class to which
they aspired. Today, with most class barriers removed, it appears that persons of every station in life are driven by their
hierarchal instinct to attempt ever more impressive language. The
result has been a rapidly increasing shift from language as communication to language as a ladder of prestige. The language
ladder is always growing, with legitimate words used to describe new technology and discoveries, but also with noncommunicative jargon, gobbledygook, and bureaucratese used
primarily to impress.

Each jargon word begins as an ''in'' word restricted to a
specific group, profession, or cult. Eventually, because the group
members have contact with outsiders, the ''in'' word or buzzword loses its exclusivity and becomes incorporated into the
general language, adding another rung to the noncommunicative
ladder. At this point the special group adopts a new buzzword
for the old meaning and the process repeats itself.

> I have never been able to understand why it is that
> just because I am unintelligible nobody understands
> me.   —MILTON MAYER

I write because I enjoy communicating, and because I enjoy communicating I am frustrated when my choice of words fails to communicate. Similarly, I am frustrated when others' words fail to communicate. I favor language that expresses coherent ideas, relevant information, or understandable instructions. I do not object to the use of slang, the convenient cliché, or informal grammar as long as it communicates, but I do object to language that mystifies rather than clarifies. This desire for clarity does not prevent me from enjoying unintentional double meanings, particularly when the intention of the writer is understood.

A department store advertisement concluded: "We can't give you your money back, but if the product is not everything we say it is you may keep it."

The Times (London): "His face was a striking one and even without his clothes, people would have turned to look at him."

Wittenberg University's school paper, *The Torch,* carried this headline: SEXUAL ATMOSPHERE SCRUTINIZED: ADMINISTRATORS TOUCH MANY AREAS.

The Vancouver Sun reported: "Women compromise more than a third of Britain's work force."

A sign in a Texas restaurant window: WANTED: MAN TO WASH DISHES AND TWO WAITRESSES.

Headline in the Pocatello *State Journal:* POCATELLO MATTRESS FACTORY PLAYS IMPORTANT ROLE IN CITY'S GROWTH.

A store in Tulsa, Oklahoma, posted this sign: LADIES ROOM OUT OF ORDER. PLEASE USE STAIRWAY.

Canton, Ohio, *Repository* headline: KEY WITNESS TAKES FIFTH
IN LIQUOR PROBE.

And a headline in the Gloversville (New York) *Herald* announced: CHOIR DIRECTOR SHOWS HIS ORGAN TO NEW CHURCH
WOMEN.

Early in my teaching career I lived and worked in a small
town and subscribed to the local newspaper. The paper was fun
to read because its many typographical errors added humor to
otherwise dull copy. Upon the return of a local sportsman from
a northern big-game hunt, the paper credited him with "bagging
a beautiful mouse." A picture of me playing in an international
chess tournament carried the caption "Artificial Insemination
Society Wants More Activity," while the cattle breeders' association had the heading "Chess Team Plays at Border." When
the president of a large pulp and paper company was scheduled
to speak at the local Chamber of Commerce, a headline announced: "Pulp Head to Address Chamber." The paper was
produced by the local printshop and regularly carried an advertising slogan across the bottom of the front page: "Our Work-
manship Speaks for Itself."
An explanation of typographical errors appeared in the Du-
buque *Witness:*

> In an ordinary newspaper column there are 10,000
> letters and there are seven wrong positions for each let-
> ter, making 70,000 chances to make errors and several
> million chances for transpositions. Next, consider the
> number of columns in each paper. . . . Did you know
> that in this sentence: "To be or not to be," by transpo-
> sition, 759,022 errors can be made?

These odds and the human propensity for error make a certain
number of mistakes inevitable. The most competent persons
throughout history have had their lapses, written something stu-

pid, or made faux pas. Conversely, the habitually incompetent have been right once in a while just by random action. This sobering thought should be a warning not to take the occasional minor error too seriously.

Although hierarchiology is primarily concerned with escalation of language to its level of incompetence, we are going to look at a few examples ranging from minor defects to major noncommunications. You will notice that some of the following typos or poor word choices only add a note of humor, while others produce unintelligible communication.

The *Kansas Bulletin:* "Our paper carried the notice last week that Mr. Hamilton Ferris is a defective in the police force. This was a typographical error. Mr. Ferris is a detective in the police farce."

An ad in the real estate section of a San Fernando Valley newspaper read: "Luxury Homes Everyone Can Afford. For Complete Details, Call Repossession Department."

The *Arkansas Democrat* carried an ad for a Little Rock department store which featured a pantie girdle: "Choose it in white or black, for a line that is sleek from waist to thing."

From the *Farmer's Digest:* "These retailers know that good beef is one of the best magnets for drawing customers into their stores, and they're not sparing the horses to get it."

Charles Reilly, executive director of the National Catholic Office for Radio and Television, wanted to promote religion with spot advertising. In an article in *Newsday,* Reilly said, "Sunday is no time for God; God ought to be in prime time."

A Massachusetts paper printed: "The fund has a deficit of $57,000 which will be used to pay teachers' salaries."

The Voice of America sent the following to its editors: "Disregard the message sent asking you to disregard NAT-2 because NAT-2 was not sent. Thus you are asked to disregard the message sent asking you to disregard the last message."

The *Dundee Courier* (Scotland): "During questions to the Prime Minister in the Commons yesterday, two youths were ejected from the Strangers' Gallery for shouting something inaudible."

A Liverpool paper wrote: "Unfortunately, the Prime Minister had left before the debate began. Otherwise he would have heard some caustic comments on his absence."

A sentence from *The Elements of Style* by Strunk and White: "The subject of a sentence and the principal verb should not, as a rule, be separated by a phrase or clause that can be transferred to the beginning."

In recent years there has been a marked increase in the use of euphemistic language to disguise things that might otherwise sound offensive. Unwanted or ill pets are "put to sleep." Funeral homes have "slumber rooms"—an innocent enough term unless you try to wake up the occupants. The real communication problems occur when language is used to conceal reality from those who have a right to know. The Park Service doesn't want to tell us it is going to kill the burros in the Grand Canyon, so it talks about "direct reduction." CIA documents contain phrases such as "termination with extreme prejudice" as a euphemism for assassination. Police label riot control "confrontation management," and the National Hot Dog and Sausage Council has ruled that the term *foot-long* may be applied to any frank exceeding eight inches.

The National Council of Teachers of English presents annual Doublespeak Awards to American public figures and business and government agencies for meretricious service in duping, gulling, confusing and hoodwinking the citizens. This tribute to those who have perpetrated language that is grossly deceptive, evasive, euphemistic, confusing, or self-contradictory has been awarded each year since 1974.

William Lutz of Rutgers University, chairman of the Committee on Public Doublespeak announced the winners of the 1983 Doublespeak Awards. The top prize went to Ronald Reagan, cited for three contributons: his naming of the MX missile "Peacemaker," his explanation that "a vote against MX production is a vote against arms control tomorrow," and his statement to the national assembly of Costa Rica that a nation that "destabilizes its neighbors by protecting guerrillas and exporting violence should forfeit close and fruitful relations with any people who truly love peace and freedom."

Second prize went to Colonel Frank Horton, commander of the air force base at Grand Forks, North Dakota, for his description of the Titan II missile that packs the top megatonnage. "It is a very large, potentially disruptive reentry system," said the colonel.

The Cleveland-based accounting firm of Ernst & Whinney came in third for its renaming of the parts of a building in an effort to obtain tax credits for a client. A fire alarm became a "combustion enunciator," and fifty-foot-high shopping-center signs became "identifying devices."

A past winner was the Pentagon for its reference to the neutron bomb as a "radiation enhancement device." The Council also found that no one in the Department of Defense could define "national security."

In the Pentagon, a war is called "defense" or a "police action"; weapons are "precision devices"; when we kill our own personnel they are called "friendly casualties"; bullets are "kinetic energy penetrators"; bombing is called "limited air interdiction" or "air support"; retreat is called "tactical deployment"; and defoliation is defined as "killing off hostile vegetation."

In a story on automated banking, *Credit and Financial Management Magazine* said, "It won't be long before customers will be able to complete most of their banking transactions without any personal contact. This will enable banks to offer more personalized services."

The *Sonoma County Realtor* advised real estate salesmen, "Don't say down payment; say initial investment. Don't ask for a listing; ask for an authorization to sell. Don't say second mortgage, say perhaps we can secure additional financing. Don't use the word contract; have them sign a proposal or offer."

According to the Internal Revenue Service, "revenue enhancement" is a tax increase, a "user fee" is a tax, "recapture of excess benefits" means taxing Social Security benefit payments. A special group may receive a "necessary tax incentive," which to others is a loophole.

Montreal, Quebec: The 450 members of the Corporation of Funeral Directors and Embalmers of Quebec changed the name of their organization to Corporation of Thanatologists—from the Greek thanatology meaning the study of death. They said, "In 20 years it will be as familiar as butcher or baker."

Bureaucrats find it hard to measure what they do, and so they generate quantities of verbiage to prove their value and protect their derrieres. In bureaucratese, nouns become verbs to emphasize activity rather than meaning, as in *prioritize, strategize, effectuate,* and *functionalize.*

The bureaucrat and the seasoned politician each acquires a special language, but there is considerable overlap. Therefore, the following small sample will include words from both. You will note that bureaucratese develops from the creation of new words and from attaching new meanings to old words. An example of a new word is *marginalized.* A bureaucrat who is not receiving his or her quota of memos is being "marginalized"—

that is, excluded from the communication hierarchy. This causes the victim of marginalization a great deal of anxiety because it means "they" would prefer that he or she be replaced, transferred to another bureaucracy, or fired. The bureaucratic meaning of *acceptable* illustrates a new meaning from an old word. *Acceptable,* to a bureaucrat, means that the right people are protected, as in "acceptable level of unemployment"—meaning our jobs are protected—or "acceptable budget"—meaning some people will get hurt, but not us.

aggression: military term describing enemy invasion of a neutral territory. The word *incursion* is preferred when we do the same thing.

alarmist: anyone who discovers an irregularity

back channel: unofficial routing of information

bafflegab: an in-house term for bureaucratese

bald eagle it: to make an appeal to patriotism as a cover for indiscretion or dishonesty. A politician may bald eagle it by claiming, "I did it in the national interest."

birdwatchers: in-house term for environmentalists or other concerned citizens

chips: concessions made to get a legislative bill passed; the basis of House or Senate wheeling and dealing

cohabitor: social welfare term for live-in sex partner

controversial: a word used by politicians when addressing the public, to avoid taking a stand on an issue that they oppose and will eventually vote against. Bureaucrats use the word simply to justify their indecisiveness.

counter-factual propositions: lies

deprived elements: social welfare term for poor people

dippers (also **double dippers**): government employees receiving two or more tax-supported incomes; usually retired military officers

downward readjustment: depression

fuzzistics: the art of being deliberately vague and dodging the real issues

Human Resources Department: unemployment office

ICE: Incidental Company Expenses; a phrase used by business and government to describe padding of the expense account

inexactitudes: lies

inoperative: A lie has been exposed.

optimize: to increase complexity so as to provide a high level of self-protection. When a bureaucrat says, "Optimize communication," he or she means: Employ language to confuse, conceal, and evade the issue.

papering the file: adding memos or other documents to the file in order to protect self and blame others; also, any action to achieve this end

plan ahead: plan

point in time: a general phrase used to evade responsibility, as in: "At that point in time there was no official policy covering that case."

profundicate: to present simple concepts in impressive academic language

residuate: to achieve a low profile in an attempt to gain an immovable position. Bureaucrats *residuate* as a survival technique during changes of administration.

retroanalyze: to go back and reexamine a project that produces positive results and discover that you had a much greater participation than previously recognized; conversely, with projects that failed, to find that your participation was minimal

selected out: fired

stimulus impoverishment: social welfare term for loneliness

toga: bureaucratic shorthand for: To get along, go along.

A House armed services committee asked the Department of Defense for a copy of the standard forms used at the Pentagon. They received 11,116 forms.

The Office of Management and Budget reported that 25 percent of state highway planning costs are incurred by paperwork.

Combined U.S. intelligence agencies dispose of one hundred tons of classified wastepaper per day.

The Paperwork Reduction Act of 1980 requires an additional paragraph to be added to the bottom of government forms explaining the act's requirements.

Congressman Jim Santini (Democrat of Nevada) estimated that if federal rules and regulations were understandable, one out of five government jobs would be eliminated and thousands of lawyers would be out of work.

The California Department of Consumer Affairs began a recent publication with a disclaimer: "For the purposes of the rules and regulations contained in this chapter, the present tense includes the past and future tenses, and the future, the present; the masculine gender includes the feminine, and the feminine, the masculine; the singular includes the plural, and the plural the singular."

A regulation of the Securities and Exchange Commission read: "Where any item calls for information with respect to any matter to be acted upon and such matter involves other matters with respect to which information is called for by other items of this schedule, the information called for by such other items shall also be given."

I. E. Solberg, member of the North Dakota state senate may have had his tongue in his cheek when he said: "What we ought to do now, obviously, is suspend all activity until we can hold a plebescite to select a panel that will appoint a commission authorized to hire a new team of experts to restudy the feasibility of compiling an index of all the committees that have in the past inventoried and catalogued the various studies aimed at finding out what happened to all the policies that were scrapped when new policies were decided on by somebody else. Once that's out of the way, I think we could go full steam ahead with some preliminary plans for a new study with Federal funds of why nothing can be done right now.''

Language is power. It grants admittance to or exclusion from many fields. George Bernard Shaw wrote, ''Every profession is a conspiracy against the layman.'' The quest for prestige involves the adoption of the language of power at the expense of real communication. The problem with this status language is that it is seldom comprehended by the reader and may be only vaguely understood by its writer, but that does not deter us from building an ever-rising hierarchy of noncommunication. As we climb this language hierarchy we reach various levels of communicative incompetence. As words lose their meaning they lose their value, and the ideas they represent also lose their value. If this continues, citizens will not be able to communicate with their government representatives. Social stratification and alienation will increase. Groups will become isolated when they cannot communicate across impassable boundaries of indecipherable vernacular, and individuals will become aliens in their own land.

COROLLARY 15: Up, up, and oops!

7

Military Intelligence

Military intelligence is a contradiction in terms.
—GROUCHO MARX

In education and the military, the Peter Principle is found in its purest form, because these hierarchies have clearly defined ranks or grades which constitute the promotion ladder. Advancement within the military is based on the old adage "You have to learn how to follow in order to lead." How can the ability to lead depend on the ability to follow? You might as well say that the ability to swim depends on the ability to sink. The greatest leaders throughout history have been notoriously poor followers.

Good followers carry out decisions made by others. Any decisions they make on their own interfere with their ability to follow. An example of good followership is provided by Andy Anderson of Marina, California. While stationed in Taiwan, he tested his officers with this communiqué: "The attached memo was circulated within the department by mistake. Section leaders are instructed to erase their initials and initial the erasure. Capt. Anderson." In a letter he later stated, "The section leaders did as instructed, no questions asked."

Occasionally a good follower, while in a low rank or when a student in a military academy, is promoted to become a good leader, but the good follower is frequently observed continuing

125

to be a good follower at whatever level of authority he or she
attains.

> I feel a fundamental crippling incuriousness about our
> officers. Too much body and too little head.
>   —T. E. LAWRENCE

Conversely, some of the greatest leaders throughout history
have been notoriously poor followers. Good followers are competent at carrying out orders, while good leaders are competent
at making decisions and giving orders.

Field Marshall Bernard Montgomery was one of the outstanding Allied commanders in World War II. He stubbornly did
things his way, but when the war was going very badly for the
British, Winston Churchill decided Montgomery's military leadership was needed. In 1942, Montgomery was appointed commander of the British 8th Army, which had just been defeated
by German General Erwin Rommel in North Africa. Montgomery proved to be an exceptional leader. He restored morale, built
up a superiority in men and equipment, and forced Rommel to
retreat across North Africa to surrender in Tunisia.

In a series of victories that ensued, culminating in acceptance of the surrender of the German northern armies on May
4, 1945, Montgomery followed a consistent policy of thorough
readiness. This policy yielded slow but steady progress and en-
sured his popularity with the men. He was frequently criticized
for overpreparedness, but he didn't move until he was good and
ready. When he came under the command of General Dwight
D. Eisenhower, there were many personal and policy conflicts.
Throughout his career, Montgomery proved to be a poor follower and a great leader.

History shows that in emergencies, when a leader falls, it is
the decisive, independent, courageous individual who steps forward, takes charge, repulses the enemy, and leads his comrades
to safety. Those with this degree of independence, initiative, and
leadership potential have a better chance of being promoted in

the field than through normal channels, or during peacetime.

There is a long tradition of competent individuals achieving failure when they reach major decision-making levels. Marcus Licinius Crassus was born in 115 B.C. and proved to be competent in business, politics, and the military while working cooperatively with others. In 54 B.C. as a Roman general, he led thousands of soldiers to their death when he was defeated in an attempt to gain military glory in an unwarranted invasion of Parthia. He was captured and executed by having molten gold poured down his throat.

Former junior army officer John Frémont, because he was a renowned frontier explorer, re-joined the Union Army in 1861 as a major general. He suffered a series of defeats by the much smaller Confederate Army in the Shenandoah Valley and resigned in 1864. He never won a battle.

Aleksei Kuropatkin was a brilliant Russian staff officer who was promoted to the rank of general. In 1904, at the beginning of the Russo-Japanese war, Kuropatkin was awarded command of the Russian Army in Manchuria. He lost every battle during the year he led the army, and was relieved of his command in 1905.

> The nature of military incompetence and those characteristics which distinguish competent from incompetent senior commanders, have shown a significant lack of variation over the years, despite changes in the other factors which shape the course of history.
>
> Whether they are well equipped or ill equipped, whether they are in control of men who are armed with spears or men with tanks and rockets, whether they are English, Russian, German, Zulu, American or French, good commanders remain pretty much the same. Likewise, bad commanders have much in common with each other.
>
> —NORMAN F. DIXON, *On the Psychology of Military Incompetence*

The medical and psychological problems that result when a competent follower is promoted were reported by Dr. R. Brown, Department of Psychiatry, National Defence Medical Centre, Ottawa, Canada, in a paper, "The Obsessive Compulsive Personality in the Canadian Forces" (published in the *Medical Services Journal, Canada,* Volume XX, Number 11). His findings apply far beyond the military establishment. Some of the outstanding characteristics of the obsessive compulsive type of person—which make for good followership—are conscientiousness, love of order, reliability, discipline, persistence, punctuality, precision, dependability, and a capacity for self-effacement. A person with mild obsessional traits is most at home in a world in which order prevails and is frequently encountered in the ranks of the civil service. Dr. Brown concludes: "Many obsessionals break down temporarily when over-promoted or when given work of an unfamiliar nature." This condition was referred to as "promotion neurosis."

> The British Soldier can stand up to anything except
> the British War Office. —GEORGE BERNARD SHAW

In a cold war, a nation voluntarily decides to take on an opponent and to match or exceed its military potential. Cold war involves sacrificing material resources, industrial output, and human potential to your opponent. Resources are committed to the opponent when they are diverted from other purposes, whether to be stockpiled or held in readiness. In the present military competitiveness between the United States and the Soviet Union, it appears that each is bent on bankrupting the other. The victor in this type of nonshooting conflict, in destroying the economy of its opponent, has sacrificed its own domestic economy to the degree that it is also impoverished—a no-win situation.

In a hot war, the object is to deliver energy sources to the enemy in order to destroy *its* resources. In olden times, when men and land were a country's main assets, winning a war paid off. Defeated armies were taken as slaves and their captured territory occupied. Today, the battle winner's resources are usually exhausted and the loser makes great economic strides.

COROLLARY 16: The higher you go the deeper you get.

Under present conditions, the only sane defense policy would be to make international law effective. Since this is not the policy of any major world power, we must evaluate military competence as the ability to wage war, even though in this nuclear age—where overkill of the world's population is a possibility—security cannot be achieved through ever-higher levels of potential mutual destruction. In the following brief review we will look at some of the people, money, and things involved in military actions.

> With 2,000 years of examples behind us we have no excuse, when fighting, for not fighting well.
> —T. E. LAWRENCE

PEOPLE

The decisions made by military leaders are highly relevant to military success or failure and are therefore a major focus of our concern. Of course, competence at all levels has its influence. No one would deny the ineptitude of the sentry who failed to recognize, and therefore killed, General Stonewall Jackson as he returned to his Confederate camp from scouting the area to formulate a battle plan.

It would be difficult to find a clearer case of incompetence than that of R. E. de Bruyeker. In 1976, while spying on behalf of the Soviet Union, he broke into the NATO naval base in Agnano, near Naples, and escaped with some secret documents. He failed to cover his tracks when he left his overnight bag in the NATO office. It contained not only the tools of his trade—a hammer, a file, and a copy of *Playboy*—but also full details about himself, including his address. He was traced very quickly.

Top marks for ineffectiveness go to Colonel John Finnis, a British Army commander in India. In 1857 he was killed by his own men just after he had lectured them on insubordination.

> Frankly we would welcome an attack. . . . We are ready for anything they may start. . . . The British Army is the finest equipped army in the world.
> —General EDMUND IRONSIDE, 1940

> Their [the Germans'] success could easily have been prevented but for the opportunities presented to them by the Allied blunders—blunders that were largely due to the prevalence of out-of-date ideas.
> —LIDDELL HART, 1940

Leadership is the capacity to make correct decisions, to show the way, and to command. A wrong decision can result from faulty mental processes or from failing to obtain accurate information.

We may never know if Edgar Allan Poe's discharge from West Point was an example of competence or incompetence unless we know the objective of his action. In 1831 the cadets were ordered to wear "white belts and gloves, under arms," for parade. Poe was expelled for "gross neglect of duty" when he arrived in the nude except for his white belts, gloves, and rifle.

In the War of 1812, the American general William Henry Winder, in spite of having a four-to-one troop superiority over the British, led his men to defeat at the battle of Stony Creek and was taken prisoner. The British realized that Winder's incompetence as a leader made him an ideal opponent, so they exchanged him, in the hope he would continue to create disasters for the Americans. Their trust was well placed. While Winder was in charge of defending the nation's capital it was raided and much of it burned to the ground.

. . . just after he had lectured them on insubordination.

Ugo Mamolo was drafted into the U.S. Army in 1959. "I didn't speak much English," said the Italian citizen, "so they made a clerk-typist out of me."

U.S. commanding officers write annual reports on officers under them. Here are some actual excerpts from evaluations:

- This officer has talents but has kept them well hidden.
- Can express a sentence in two paragraphs any time.
- A quiet, reticent officer. Industrious, tenacious, careful and neat. I do not wish to have this officer as a member of my command at any time.
- Is keenly analytical and his highly developed mentality could best be utilized in the research and development field. He lacks common sense.

The Duke of Medina Sidonia was promoted to the command of the Spanish Armada in 1588. He wrote to the king: "My health is bad, and from my small experience of the water I know that I am always seasick. The commander of such a vast, vitally important expedition ought to understand navigation and naval warfare; I know nothing of either. If you send me, depend upon it, I shall have a bad account to render of my trust.'' Phillip II sent him anyway!

In 1948, Colonel David Marcus of the Israeli Army was killed by his own soldiers because they thought he was an Arab. He was urinating outside his tent, with a bedsheet wrapped around him, at the time.

Aleksander Samsonov was an indifferent Russian bureaucrat promoted to general in command of the Russian 2nd Army in World War I. He was an outstanding incompetent. He could not find the enemy, but the Germans found him at Tanenberg and slaughtered his troops. He was so embarrassed that he tried to get killed by riding into the line of attack, but failed. His persistence eventually paid off and he managed to commit suicide successfully.

Following the World War I battle of Verdun, General Robert Nivelle assumed command of the French armies on the Western Front. He decided to mount another great offensive and ordered masses of troops to the front, causing thousands of useless and unnecessary deaths. The soldiers finally mutinied and Nivelle was dismissed.

In 1956, a Marine Corps drill sergeant at Parris Island boot camp ordered a platoon of recruits to march into water over their heads. Six drowned because they couldn't swim.

> Competence, then, is the free exercise of dexterity
> and intelligence in the completion of tasks, unim-
> paired by infantile inferiority.   —E. H. ERIKSON

A Japanese soldier, Lieutenant Hiroo Onoda, fought World War II until March 1974. The lack of armed opposition after 1945 did not deter him from defending the remote island in the Philippines where he was stationed. Neither did the letters dropped from the air, requesting him to come home, lessen his determination. He thought it was a Yankee trick to get him to surrender, so he continued to come out of the jungle occasionally and fire a warning shot on behalf of the Emperor. When he was found in 1974 and returned to Japan, it took six months to convince him the war was over.

Antonio López de Santa Anna patterned his life after his hero, Napoleon, and considered himself a great tactician. In spite of copying Napoleon's hairstyle, combing his hair from the back of his head to his forehead, he failed to look like Napoleon, who was short and fat while Antonio was tall and skinny. Further, Santa Anna had only one leg. The other had been put to rest in a special burial service at a Santa Paula cemetery after he lost it fighting the French in 1838.

Despite his hero worship he lacked Napoleon's strategic gifts. In a maneuver to confuse the enemy, he dressed his troops in the enemy's uniforms and then made a surprise attack. The result was total confusion and complete failure.

The high point of his career was the twelve-day siege, February 23 to March 6, 1836, on the former Franciscan mission known as the Alamo in San Antonio, Texas. Santa Anna, with four thousand Mexican troops, killed all of the less than two hundred Texas volunteers defending the Alamo.

Sam Houston, commander of the army, rallied his troops with the cry "Remember the Alamo!" In a show of confidence on April 20, 1836, Santa Anna made camp at the San Jacinto River, next to where the Texans were known to be hiding, and commanded his men to have a siesta. Early the next morning his entire army was wiped out in just eighteen minutes. When Santa Anna was roused from his sleep by the noise of the attack, he shouted, "The enemy is upon us," and left on horseback. In the Mexican War, 1846–1848, he lost every battle he fought.

During the Kennedy administration, an order was made to devise an evacuation plan in case of nuclear attack. Unbeknownst to Kennedy, two plans were made. One gave priority to Pentagon generals and was shown to the Joint Chiefs of Staff. The other gave priority to civilians and was presented to the Cabinet. Because the two plans were top secret, neither group knew of the other plan. Had there been an alert, confusion would have been monumental. The man who wrote the plans put himself near the top of both lists.

On October 25, 1854, James Thomas Brudenell led a charge of British cavalry against the Russians at Balaklava during the Crimean War. The story of what happened was immortalized in Alfred Lord Tennyson's poem "The Charge of the Light Brigade." Brudenell, a quarrelsome martinet who had purchased most of his promotions, made his cavalrymen the best dressed in the service by spending large sums of his own money. At Balaklava he received ambiguous orders, and although he questioned their meaning, he acted on them and charged in the wrong direction and toward the wrong units. The attack took place not against a weakened flank, as planned, but against the most fortified center position of enemy lines, resulting in the loss of more than 268 of the 670 soldiers, cut down by Russian artillery. Brudenell was slightly wounded and left the battlefield while his men were still fighting. The futile gallantry of the charge captured the imagination of the British public and he was lionized on his return to England.

> In a situation where the consequences of wrong decisions are so awesome, where a single bit of irrationality can set a whole train of traumatic events in motion, I do not think that we can be satisfied with the assurance that most people behave rationally most of the time.   —C. E. OSGOOD

A six-man army team was airlifted to Brownsville, Texas, on a secret training exercise. Equipped with machine guns, the unit was assigned to get in and out of the city without being seen. The unit got lost, however, and ended up asking a farmer for help. The farmer phoned the sheriff, who said he could transport them to town. The radio dispatch summoning deputies to the farmhouse was monitored by Brownsville reporter Don Arnwine, who went to investigate. Arnwine snapped photos of the unit as they got out of the police cars. A deputy demanded the film for reasons of "national security." Despite the deputy's threats, the aborted "secret" mission made front-page news in Brownsville and the national wire services.

> An intelligence service is, in fact, a stupidity service. —E. B. WHITE

> Our present ratio of support to combat forces is greater than five to one. . . . Our existing armed forces now have more admirals and generals, captains and colonels, than at the height of World War II when there were more than 12 million men under arms. We have one commissioned or non-commissioned officer for every enlisted man!
> —HERBERT SCOVILL, JR., former deputy director of the CIA

> The army currently has more lieutenant colonels assigned to personnel management (903) than to leading infantry (838). And twice as many in Material Management (1,148) as in artillery command (547).
> —*Washington Monthly*

Speaking on nuclear war, T. K. Jones, Deputy Undersecretary of Defense for Strategic and Theater Nuclear Forces, suggested: "Dig a hole, cover it with a couple of doors and then throw three feet of dirt on top. . . . It's the dirt that does it. . . . If there are enough shovels to go around, everybody's going to make it."

> War is much too serious a matter to be trusted to the
> military.   —TALLEYRAND

The Thanh Hoa bridge, ninety miles south of Hanoi, was a key air force target during the Vietnam War. Bombing was ordered when air force officers determined that the bridge was a key supply conduit for the North Vietnamese. The North Vietnamese claimed to have shot down more than one hundred aircraft attempting to bomb the bridge, but in May 1972 it was finally destroyed. The North Vietnamese had been fording supplies across the river about five miles downstream for years.

> Not since the Inchon landing has a U.S. military venture been crowned by success. Our military performance since 1950 suggests that we as a society have lost touch with the art of war. Inchon was followed by the rout of American forces along the Yalu, Yalu by the Bay of Pigs fiasco, the Bay of Pigs by the disaster in Indochina, Indochina by the fizzled raid on Son Toy to retrieve U.S. POWs thought to be confined in North Vietnam, Son Toy by the abortive assault on Koh Tang Island in search of the hijacked Mayaguez, and Mayaguez by the debacle in the Iranian desert.   —JEFFERY RECORD

General Andrew J. Goodpaster of The Citadel, a military college in Charleston, South Carolina, traces the deterioration among army personnel to the conflict in Vietnam with its "phony reports on resources and readiness." Although the problem is probably more complex than that, many public statements did not square with the facts.

> It is the inherent right of the Government to lie to save itself.
> —Assistant Secretary of Defense ARTHUR D. SYLVESTER, December 6, 1962

By Christmas it will all be over.
—General PAUL D. HARKINS, April 1963

We are not about to send boys nine or ten thousand
miles away from home to do what Asian boys ought
to be doing for themselves.
—President LYNDON B. JOHNSON, October 21,
1964

The Viet Cong will just peter out.
—General MAXWELL D. TAYLOR, October 27,
1965

By the end of 1967, there might be light at the end
of the tunnel and everybody will get the feeling that
things are much better.
—HENRY CABOT LODGE, U.S. ambassador to South
Vietnam, December 16, 1966

Hanoi has accepted near-total-defeat. . . . Anyone
with practical common sense should be able to see
. . . Hanoi's acceptance of near-total defeat. . . .
The numerous American politicians and thinkers who
endlessly said . . . we could never get an honorable
settlement . . . look pretty silly.
—JOSEPH ALSOP, November 1, 1972

MONEY

The world is spending a million dollars a minute on weapons; more than half of it is expended by the United States and
the Soviet Union. Already the United States and Russia possess
nuclear weapons with explosive power of 32 trillion pounds of
TNT, enough for 4 tons for every man, woman, and child on
earth, or enough for 800,000 Hiroshima-size bombs.
Arms spending continues to escalate and is the single great-

est cause of inflation. It removes natural, technological, manufacturing, and human resources from general use and places them in ever-increasing concentration in nonproductive, expensive, and ultimately destructive use, thus reducing the world's real wealth, as reflected in the declining value of currency.

In America, more than one fourth of our scientific and engineering talent is channeled into defense. This has eroded our country's ability to compete with Japan and other industrialized countries in consumer markets other than those in weapons. The most competent graduates from Japanese universities go to work on improving the quality and production of cameras, television sets, computers, and automobiles, applying their ingenuity and advanced technology to consumer products.

The escalation of American defense spending contributes to budget deficits, raising the specter of recession while further reducing our ability to compete in international markets.

The Pentagon is the largest single purchaser of goods and services in the nation. With its enormous size and budget, the Pentagon exerts power over congressmen and other officials; they support military spending because their political survival depends on it. Under these conditions the constitutional checks and balances of American government break down.

The administration's estimated $1.6 trillion military buildup will cost $20,000 for each American household over the next five years, but may actually cost much more. Escalation of costs over estimates is a military tradition that results from policy, specification changes, and incompetence.

It is policy for defense estimates to be low so that they will be approved, because it is known that once budgets are passed, increases will get through almost automatically. Defense contractors always bid low, figuring that once the contract has been secured, the government will be reluctant to incur the bother and delay of changing contractors. Defense contractor Pratt & Whitney estimated an engine part to cost $16. They later "re-priced" it at $3,033.82.

The cost of incompetence is seen at every level. The Pentagon admits that they miscalculated the cost of forty-four new weapons systems by $114.5 billion.

In a private Pentagon dining room, 126 admirals eat their lunches. The cost is $31 per lunch, and each lunch is subsidized $26.98 worth by the taxpayers.

The army reprimanded its comptroller and another general for sloppy accounting that caused an expenditure of $165 million more than Congress had authorized. Though the errors involved loss of records for the sale and delivery of equipment to foreign countries, the fiscal damage remained. The army announced it had sent letters of reprimand to the two generals.

In a six-month investigation, by the inspector general's office, of the cost of about fifteen thousand different military spare parts, it was found that two thirds of the items had risen in cost more than 50 percent between 1980 and 1982, and four thousand items had risen more than 500 percent.

A recent air force study of the skyrocketing cost of spare parts concluded they will soon be $4 billion behind in inventory.

A commonly used navy and air force contract allows increases between time of ordering and date of delivering a spare part. For example, a tube assembly ordered at $117.26 was finally delivered by Pratt & Whitney at $1,308.08, an increase of 1,016 percent.

The inspector general's report explained that in many cases the contractor is not the manufacturer, and concluded: "The price included overhead and other markup factors that would not be paid if the parts were bought directly from the actual manufacturers." This markup is responsible for a large part of the $1.8 billion expenditure for spare parts in 1981. A bolt that retails for 67 cents costs the military $17.59, and a $2.83 connector costs $57.52.

Hundreds of thousands of veterans collect military pensions while holding down other jobs. After twenty years of career military service, a retiree collects a 50 percent pension. With life expectancies rising, the amount spent annually on retired military personnel is expected to reach $28 billion per year by the year 2000.

Thirty-four years ago, two military commissions were established to protect Americans from the Nazis. The commissions, with annual combined budgets of $30,000, still meet regularly. Lieutenant Colonel John Child explains that the money goes for salaries and entertainment. "We don't have formal sessions now. The commissions meet socially after hours."

A review by the General Accounting Office of the Department of Defense's $4 billion consulting outlay revealed that more than 50 percent went to former employees. Forty percent of the consulting contracts were unsolicited.

Darius King, a veteran of the War of 1812, was discharged in 1814. In 1869, in his early seventies, he took a nineteen-year-old bride. He died eighteen years after this marriage. Mrs. King received widow's benefits through an army pension until June 1938, when she died at the age of eighty-nine. Darius King had served in the army for fifty-four days, but the benefits continued for 124 years.

Former Representative Otis Pike of New York took a small steel rod to the House floor. "In the manufacturers catalogue," Pike said, "This rod is described as a 'precision shafting.' For once, it seems, the American taxpayer got precisely what he paid for." He then announced that the 50-cent rod he held in his hand cost taxpayers $25.55.

An ancient saying goes, "There are three ways to do anything: the right way, the wrong way and the army way." The army, navy and air force still can't do things quite like everyone else. They can't go out and buy something they need even if it is a standard item available in your local supermarket or hardware store. First, elaborate "military specifications" must be drawn up. Twenty-four pages are required to list the specifications for T-shirts, fifteen pages for chewing gum, and seventeen for Worcestershire sauce. The specifications for a wood interdental stimulator (toothpick), a nut or a bolt, and the required code number are given as one reason why the price is so high. According to *Time* magazine:

Defense Department Engineer Ralph Applegate was fired six years ago for disclosing that the services were paying $1,130 apiece for piston rings that civilian buyers could purchase for as little as $100 each. Explanations are still being sought about why the Navy spent $18,000 on a couch for the officers' wardroom of one destroyer. Asked what special features made the couch so expensive, an admiral replied that officers would "use it for a long time."

The air force had to buy seventy-one aluminum ladders, ten feet long, for pilots to enter the A-10 airplane. The cost was $1,676 each. A ten-foot ladder at most hardware stores sold for less than $100.

Steward Storm, a retired navy man now working for the government in Washington, investigated the enormous difference in civilian and military cost of standard items. He found that the military user of an item usually had no idea of its cost, because the purchaser and the user were kept apart, in separate departments. This situation, for example, made it possible for the Sperry Corporation to charge the navy $110 each for diodes that could be purchased wholesale for 4 cents. To make his point he went to a Radio Shack retail outlet and bought a package of ten of the navy $110 diodes for 99 cents.

The navy wanted to order 1,366 new F/A-18 Hornet aircraft at a cost of $41 billion, or $30 million each—which is triple the $9.9 million originally projected. The aircraft burned fuel so fast in test flights that its combat range will be only about 390 miles, which means that carriers will have to sail closer to hostile shores than desirable. Other tests have revealed that its air-to-ground radar is "grossly inaccurate," as well as other inadequacies. The navy is now considering cutting back its orders—which will drive the cost of individual planes still higher—and substituting for the unpurchased Hornets some even more expensive F-14 Tomcats at $44.3 million each.

1952	Russia spent $34 billion on arms America spent $43 billion
1960	Russia spent $33 billion America spent $45 billion
1965	Russia spent $45 billion America spent $52 billion
1970	Russia $63 billion America spent $78 billion
1980	Russia upped the ante to over $100 billion America saw that and raised to $126 billion

President Reagan asked Congress for a 1984 defense budget of $274 billion and proposed a five-year, $2 trillion military spending plan.

> The only way we can win the arms race with the Soviets is if they go broke first.   —ART BUCHWALD

THINGS

Weapons and other military equipment also demonstrate a tendency to reach levels of incompetence. It is recorded that in

1628 the largest naval vessel of its time, the *Vasa,* a Swedish battleship, was launched. Not only was it the biggest, but it had the most guns: sixty-four cannons on two decks. It sank immediately because it was top-heavy.

Germany won the 1870 battle of Sedan over the French because of the superiority of its steel guns, which were manufactured by Alfred Krupp. The French used bronze guns. Before the war, Krupps' frequent solicitations to secure orders from French officers were stamped "No action required."

A spectacular British World War II contribution to weapon incompetence was the No. 74 (ST) hand grenade, nicknamed the sticky bomb. It had three unique features: (1) An adhesive coating enabled it to stick to an enemy tank. Unfortunately, this also enabled it to stick to the thrower. (2) Its four-and-a-half-pound weight made it extremely difficult for a soldier to lob it far enough to ensure his own safety. (3) Its five-second delay—even if the improbable happened and a hit was made and it stuck to the tank—was hardly long enough for the soldier to remove himself from the scene of action.

The governor of Utah, Scott M. Matheson, protested the storing of nerve gas—enough to kill the entire population of the world forty-two times—at the Tooele Army Depot only thirty miles from Salt Lake City. The gas is stored in concrete "igloos" along an earthquake fault line. The Defense Department agreed to neutralize the gas in 1972, but apparently no action has been taken and plans to ship tons more continue. Weteye nerve gas is so deadly that one shell can destroy life for thousands of square miles. It is invisible, odorless, and tasteless, and kills in fourteen seconds. There is no known antidote.

The $2.7 million M-1 tank has a 63 percent chance of engine failure within the first 4,000 miles of use. The tank treads last 1,056 miles and the tank requires 1.34 worker-hours of maintenance time for each hour of operation. When the Chrysler Corporation was told the army was considering having another company build the tanks, a spokesman declared, "Chrysler Corporation has developed and engineered a superb new battle tank."

General Charles F. Kuyk told *The Wall Street Journal* that he was pleased with the C-5A cargo plane. Even though, he confessed, "Having the wings fall off at 8,000 hours is a problem."

The United States spent $2 million during World War II to develop bat bombs. The plan, brainstorm of Pennsylvania dental surgeon Lytle S. Adams, called for bombs with timers to be surgically wired to bats. The bats would be dropped from a plane over Japan, seek refuge under eaves, and explode, setting off fires. Production of as many as a million bat bombs were to begin production in March of 1944. The chief of naval operations halted the program because the behavior of the bats, once freed, was "uncertain."

The navy spent four years and $375,000 investigating military applications for the Frisbee. The scientists of the Naval Air Command attempted to produce "an air-launch illuminations system using a gyroscopically stabilized disc." Their plans were scuttled when the navy discovered that Frisbees wouldn't always go where you want them to.

The army wanted a truck that would go where there were no roads. An aerospace contractor, Ling-Temco-Vought, came up with an idea that the army liked: the Gamma Goat, a small amphibious vehicle that could be parachuted from a plane.

During its development, the cost of the Goat rose from $69 million to $439 million and the vehicle grew from Jeep size to a 7.5-ton monster. It was completed three years after its projected date. Brigadier General Vincent Ellis, the Army's procurement deputy, said that he was pleased with the results.

Senator William Proxmire, whose Joint Economic Subcommittee investigates cost overruns, told General Ellis, in part: "You have a program that is three years late. You have a truck that is three times heavier than it was supposed to be and does not have a bigger payload, and one that is twice as expensive as the original estimate. It seems to me that you are an easy man to please."

In describing the Gamma Goat, Elmer Staats, U.S. Comptroller General, said that it is a prominent example of buying something before you really know what you want.

During the Franco-Prussian War, so great was the secrecy surrounding the new weapon, the *mitrailleuse* or machine gun, that no instructions were issued on how to work it.

In 1917 the British Navy built a number of K-boats, which they hoped would assure victory. The steam-powered submarines did not fare as well as anticipated. No. 2 caught fire on its first dive. No. 3 sank with the Prince of Wales on board. It was salvaged, only to be rammed by no. 6 and sunk. No. 4 ran aground. No. 5 sank, losing all hands. No. 7 rammed no. 17 and was scrapped. No. 14 sprang a leak while still docked, but later rammed no. 22 and sank. During sea trials, no. 17 rammed a cruiser and sank. No. 22 was rammed by an escort cruiser. The project was discontinued in 1918.

At the beginning of World War II the Russians devised a plan to destroy German tanks. These disciples of Pavlov trained dogs to associate food with the bottom of tanks. Thus, they reasoned, the dogs would run under the attacking panzers with bombs strapped to their backs and destroy the enemy tanks. The unexpected turn of events was that the dogs associated food only with Russian tanks. Soviet tanks were forced to retreat as the bomb-bearing dogs ran toward them.

An excerpt from army regulations 135–300: "Tent pegs . . . must be painted orange. The bright color provides an easy means of locating the pegs. . . . When bright orange pegs are used, they must be driven into the ground completely out of sight.''

To compensate for the weight of all the latest radar, missiles, and computerized combat-information centers, the navy built ships with aluminum superstructures instead of steel, thus reducing the weight by 5 percent and cutting construction costs by 2 percent. Unfortunately, aluminum burns. In 1975 the U.S. cruiser *Belknap* collided with the aircraft carrier *John F. Kennedy*. The *Belknap* burned to the gunwales and took more than four years to rebuild.

According to a report from the General Accounting Office, the army got the Pershing II missile to hit the target by ''altering the target area by placing aluminum reflectors in a precise geometrical pattern to insure that the target had a distinctive radar signature.''

The army expects to spend $13.4 billion over the next several years to acquire 6,882 Bradley Fighting Vehicles, even though each one could be knocked out by a single M-42 grenade which costs $2. The aluminum tank vaporizes and becomes a fireball when hit by a grenade.

In 1970 the army rejected an early version of the tank because it was too expensive at $151,000 each. But in 1977 the Bradley was approved at a cost of $338,000 per vehicle. By 1982 the price had escalated to $1.94 million each.

The tank features a five-hundred-horsepower diesel engine that gets two miles to the gallon; a driver's hatch positioned so the driver cannot see where he is going when he makes a right turn; a flotation collar which, when it was demonstrated in 1980 at Fort Knox, did not support the tank, leaving it to sink in the Ohio River; a missile launcher that takes two and a half minutes to reload. The tank is ten feet tall, making it clearly visible on the battlefield. It must be partially disassembled to fit into the standard C-141 military transport plane, and it must come to a complete stop to fire its antitank missile.

In 1980 an integrated circuit chip the size of a dime was twice responsible for putting America on nuclear alert. The three-minute alert was enough for an unarmed command and control plane to be in the air before the military realized no bombs were headed our way. Pentagon technicians replaced a faulty circuit chip worth 46 cents which had relayed the misinformation from a computer below Colorado's Cheyenne Mountains to command centers around the country.

Another false alarm lasted about six minutes when the same computer was inaccurately fed information simulating conditions of a nuclear attack.

> The basic problems facing the world today are not susceptible to a military solution.
> —JOHN F. KENNEDY

8

Short Cuts

But be not afraid of greatness: some men are born great,
some achieve greatness, and some have greatness thrust upon
them.   —WILLIAM SHAKESPEARE

And some are born incompetent, some achieve incompetence,
and some have incompetence thrust upon them. It may be that
Cal Luss, the metallurgist at Akme Lead and Pewter Products,
was actually incompetent before he was born, but it only became evident at his birth. Mr. and Mrs. Luss had hoped for a
girl, and Cal's lifelong difficulty getting along with people had
its beginning when, by being the wrong sex, he failed to satisfy
his parents.

> COROLLARY 17: Incompetence knows no barriers of time or
> place.

One can think of many inborn defects that ultimately produce incompetence. Stu Pidd, the foreman of Akme, was probably endowed with a genetic limitation of his intellectual capability
and therefore could be said to have been born to become incompetent.

The world of the future will be an ever more de-
manding struggle against the limitations of our
intelligence.   —NORBERT WIENER

Hy Sterik, the talented artist who found his level of incompetence in administration as advertising director at Akme, was typical of those who climb to incompetence. He had been a successful student at art school, a talented free-lance artist, and a capable commercial illustrator at Perfect Pitch Pewter. It was because of this background that he was able to achieve incompetence as an administrator.

> See how today's achievement is only tomorrow's
> confusion.   —WILLIAM DEAN HOWELLS

Jerry Attrick was competently managing Akme Lead Weight and Sinker, Inc., when the board of directors decided to expand the company's operation. It was not Jerry's idea to go into the tuning fork business and get in over his head. It can be fairly said that he had incompetence thrust upon him.

> You know I'm the result of forces beyond my
> control.   —A. R. AMMONS

There are areas of human endeavor where an individual can be an instant success or failure and avoid the long process of climbing step by step to professional fulfillment. Make a startling prediction forecasting an unforeseeable event and if the prediction comes true you will promptly be hailed as a gifted prognosticator or forecaster. In the world of entertainment you can be an unknown, but one hit record or one successful role and overnight you are a highly paid performer and celebrity. In major league sports, become a winner and immediately you are showered with fame and fortune.

SOOTHSAYERS AND TRUTHSAYERS

It is easy to predict some events accurately. For example: "You will die within one year of your last birthday." But some prognosticators are willing to take chances by forecasting events that are not inevitable. This may be a real short cut to incompetence.

> Forecasting is very difficult—especially if it is about
> the future. He who lives by the crystal ball soon learns
> to eat ground glass.   —EDGAR FIEDLER

British Parliament ordered a study of Thomas A. Edison's electric light bulb in 1878. The report concluded: "Edison's ideas are good enough for our trans-Atlantic friends, but unworthy of the attention of practical or scientific men."

> Lieutenant Joseph Ives of the U.S. Corps of Topo-
> logical Engineers declared in 1861: "The Grand Can-
> yon . . . is, of course, altogether valueless. Ours has
> been the first, and will doubtless be the last, party of
> whites to visit the profitless locality."

> Remington Arms Company was offered the patent to
> the typewriter in 1897 by the Wagner Typewriting
> Machine Company. Remington did not purchase the
> machine because, "No mere machine can replace a
> reliable and honest clerk." Underwood acquired the
> Wagner Company and sold more than 12 million
> typewriters in the fifty years that followed.

The brilliant writer H. G. Wells reached his level of incompetence as a seer in 1902. "I must confess," Wells said, "that my imagination, in spite even of spurring, refuses to see any sort of submarine doing anything but suffocating its crew and floundering at sea."

In 1912, Samuel Courtauld, a British chemist, called on the president of Lister & Co., a Yorkshire textile mill. Courtauld offered Lister the formula for rayon. Lister officiously proclaimed: "It will never catch on—the public will never accept artificial silks."

In 1930, Rear Admiral Clark Woodward of the U.S. Navy stated, "So far as sinking a ship with a bomb is concerned, you just can't do it."

On July 22, 1832, Giuseppe Verdi applied to study music at the Royal and Imperial Conservatory of Milan. Maestro Francesco Basily, the principal, rejected the boy, declaring him "certain to prove mediocre."

Paul Cezanne was attacked with these words in 1874: "Mr. Cezanne must be some kind of lunatic, afflicted with delirium tremens while he is painting."

Twenty years later, when Cezanne, among others, was acknowledged by the French government, a critic wrote: "For the state to accept such filth can only indicate moral blight."

A professor of literature at the Lycée d'Aix graded one of his students zero for composition and French literature. The student was Emile Zola.

Archbishop Hieronymous, Count Colloredo of Salzburg, heard Mozart's first great opera, *Idomeneo,* and dismissed him from his post at court, stating that he was incompetent.

After the first performance of *The Marriage of Figaro,* in Vienna in 1786, Emperor Joseph II of Bavaria offered this critique: "Far too noisy, my dear Mozart. Far too many notes."

Music critic Philip Hale of Boston wrote in 1837: "If Beethoven's Seventh Symphony is not by some means abridged, it will soon fall into disuse."

Rembrandt died a pauper in 1669, totally unrecognized as an artist. Two centuries later, John Ruskin, England's leading art critic, rendered much the same opinion as Rembrandt's contemporaries. "All the colors are wrong . . . vulgarity, dullness and impiety will always express themselves through art in brown and grays as in Rembrandt. It is the aim of the best painters to paint the noblest things they can see by sunlight. It was the aim of Rembrandt to paint the foulest things he could see by rush-light.''

> Rembrandt is not to be compared in the painting of character with our extraordinarily gifted English artist, Mr. Rippingille.   —JOHN HUNT (1775–1848)

Union General John Sedwick stood before his men in 1864 and said, ''Come, come! Why they couldn't hit an elephant at this dist—''

''We believe the boat is unsinkable,'' said the vice-president of the White Star Line, speaking of the *Titanic*. Confirming this misplaced confidence, Captain E. J. Smith avowed, ''I cannot imagine any condition which would cause this ship to flounder. I cannot conceive of any vital disaster happening to this vessel. Modern shipbuilding has gone beyond that.''

When the ship received radio warnings of icebergs in the shipping lanes, Captain Smith, hoping to set a record, confidently maintained his top speed.

Because the ship was equipped with watertight compartments, there was little more than a token number of lifeboats aboard. When the *Titanic* sideswiped an iceberg, too many compartments were ripped open. Desperate SOS signals were ignored by a nearby ship, on which the radio operator, who had been working a double shift, had turned off his radio to get some sleep. Only 705 of the *Titanic*'s 2,208 passengers and crew survived the 1912 disaster.

The city fathers of Pompeii were urged by the sibyls, prophets of the Roman empire, to evacuate the town. The leaders decided not to warn the citizenry and to stay. The sibyls fled. The next day, Mount Vesuvius buried Pompeii in ten feet of volcanic ash.

Tobacconist John Player approached E. G. Alton, president of E. G. Alton & Co., suggesting a partnership. Player wanted to produce chopped tobacco wrapped in paper. The cigar maker declined, adding, "Your cigar-ettes will never become popular."

Brian Epstein approached Dick Rose, a record executive at Decca, in 1962 with a demo of a group he was managing. Rose listened to the record but refused to sign the group, saying, "Groups with guitars are on their way out." The Beatles were also offered unsuccessfully to Columbia Records, Pye, and HMV. Later, the group went with EMI and within six years sold 100 million albums and 100 million singles for that label.

Albert Einstein, who had been rejected by the Munich Technical Institute in 1898 because he would "never amount to very much," formulated his theory of relativity in his spare time while an inspector at the Swiss patent office in Berne.

Through the fall of 1888, the Cambria Iron Company of Pennsylvania repeatedly predicted the South Fork Reservoir dam would collapse if not repaired. The wealthy South Fork Fishing and Hunting Club felt there was no danger and opposed opening the sluice gates because it would disturb the fish. On May 31, 1889, an unseasonal rain filled the lake and at 3:10 P.M. the dam gave way. The Johnstown flood killed 2,300 people.

The British Society for Psychical Research conducted ESP tests at Cambridge University in the 1890's. Their tests had all failed, when two young men, Smith and Blackburn, arrived claiming they could communicate via brain waves. Smith's eyes were bandaged, his ears plugged, and his body covered with heavy blankets. Still, he could produce words and even redraw pictures transmitted by Blackburn. The experiments were widely publicized as solid proof of ESP.

Twenty years later, Blackburn revealed how he and Smith had fooled the experts. Blackburn, with sleight of hand a magician would envy, slipped pieces of cigarette paper to Smith. Smith viewed them with a luminous stone hidden in his vest. Blackburn said he concocted the stunt to prove that scientists could be fooled into believing something if they really wanted to believe.

A book titled *Predictions for 1976* contained the following:

Psychic Daniel Logan predicted that Lucille Ball would be named ambassador to an Asian nation.

Joseph East of Chicago predicted a political movement to nominate God as President of the United States.

Dr. Joseph Jeffers predicted that the Messiah would be seen on television to give the final warning to repent before Armageddon, which he said was scheduled to begin in June, ''if not sooner.''

Edgar Cayce's most famous glimpse into the future claimed that California would break off and disappear into the ocean. Though he never gave a date, his followers said it would happen in April 1969. It was then amended to 1975, then to 1982.

Billing himself as the twentieth-century Nostradamus, Jeron King Criswell claimed to be correct 87 percent of the time. Among his spectacularly incorrect predictions:

- The first astronauts to land on the moon would be pregnant women.
- Nine women would sit on the Supreme Court by 1976.
- Richard M. Nixon would be elected to a third term as President of the United States.

Criswell was the author of a book entitled *Criswell Predicts to the Year Two Thousand.* The book forecasts the end of the world for August 18, 1999, but makes no predictions for what happens between then and the year 2000.

> You can make a better living in the world as a sooth-
> sayer than as a truthsayer. —G. C. LICHTENBERG

In April of 1974, Jeane Dixon wrote: "I know it looks bad
for President Nixon right now but I predict he will emerge successful and strengthened from the [Watergate] crisis. His name
will not be damaged. As he moves along, his credibility will
become even stronger."

> I met a prognosticator who was 100 percent correct
> about 2 percent of the time. —IRENE PETER

On October 29, 1929, the New York stock market crashed
four days after President Hoover had declared, "The fundamental business of this country . . . is on a sound and prosperous
basis."

Christopher Columbus was stranded in Jamaica in need of
supplies. He knew that an eclipse was to occur the next day,
March 1, 1504. He told the tribal chief: "The God who protects
me will punish you. Indeed, this very night his vengeance will
fall upon you and the moon shall change her color and lose her
light, in testimony of the evils which shall be sent upon you from
the skies."

When the eclipse darkened the sky, Columbus got all the
supplies he needed.

In the early 1900's, an Englishman tried the same trick on a
Sudanese chieftain. "If you do not follow my order," the official warned, "I will put big magic on you. I will bite a piece
out of the moon."

"If you are referring to the lunar eclipse," the chief replied,
"that doesn't happen until the day after tomorrow."

A chronology of prognostications about transportation:

• In 1830, Dr. Dionysius Lardner, of University College in
London, informed the world that a steamship would not be

able to cross the Atlantic because it would require more coal than the ship could hold. Eight years later, the *Great Western* steamed across the Atlantic. Dr. Lardner also said travel by steam engine would "not be possible, because passengers, unable to breathe, would die of asphyxia."

• In 1899, the Literary Digest predicted a dim future for the horseless carriage. "At present it is a luxury for the wealthy; and although its price will probably fall . . . it will never, of course, come into as common use as the bicycle."

• In 1932, Boeing's 247 made its first flight. A company engineer triumphantly declared, "There will never be a bigger plane built." The twin-engine, all-metal plane carried ten.

• In 1948, British and American executives of automotive companies toured the Volkswagen factory in Germany. Ernest Breech, executive vice-president of the Ford Motor Company, commented, "The car is not worth a damn." Sir William Rootes added a British raspberry, saying the Volkswagen did not "meet the fundamental technical requirements of a motor car."

> Prophecy, however honest, is generally a poor substitute for experience.
> —Justice BENJAMIN N. CARDOZO

NO BUSINESS LIKE SHOW BUSINESS

Examples of military, political, and business incompetence merit thoughtful consideration because the perpetrators were or are serious. In show business the criteria for incompetence are reversed. The ultimate incompetence occurs when the performers are entertaining for the wrong reasons. Often the catastrophes, happenstances, and coincidences involve entertainers who were otherwise competent performers.

Ed Sullivan liked to pay tribute to stars who were in the studio audience of his TV show. On one show he had the lights turned up and announced, "Sitting out in our audience is the talented Dolores Gray, currently starving on Broadway."

In 1959 announcer Grant J. Austin of Lima, Ohio, told his WIMA television audience: "Ladies and gentlemen, stay tuned for *Matt Basterson* next on NBC."

The high point of each performance by Janos, the Incredible Rubber Man, was when he entwined his legs behind his head and rolled around the stage. In August 1978, while appearing in Roberts Brothers Circus at Southend, England, Janos could not get himself untangled. He just sat there on stage like a human pretzel until a circus official, Kenneth Julian, had Janos put in the back of his van and taken to the hospital. It took doctors half an hour to straighten him out. They ordered Janos to lie flat for a week.

Many entertainers have areas of incompetence not directly related to their performances.

A personal problem and a public performance did come together when the great French satirist Molière was taken fatally ill while performing the role of the hypochondriac in his play *The Imaginary Invalid*.

Bronco Billy Anderson, star of the first classic American western, *The Great Train Robbery*, was not an incompetent actor just because he had to be helped into the saddle.

Bela Lugosi, star of *Dracula* and other horror movies, became faint at the sight of his own blood.

Tony Bennett, a singer of great talent and appeal, played the part of Hymie Kelly in the 1966 movie *The Oscar. Cue* magazine said: "Tony looks like a sad, abandoned bulldog."

Bob Dylan, the songwriter and singer, acted under the direction of Sam Peckinpah in the 1973 movie *Pat Garrett and Billy the Kid. Newsweek* said of his performance: "Bob Dylan twitches at the mouth in a disastrous screen debut." *Variety* said his acting is "currently limited to an embarrassing assortment of tics, smirks, shrugs, winks and smiles."

Evel Knievel, the stuntman who grabbed national attention in the seventies, played himself in the 1977 film *Viva Knievel.* Film writer Leslie Halliwell said, "Abysmal attempt to turn a stuntman into an actor; a most ramshackle vehicle."

John V. Lindsay, twice mayor of New York and former congressman, acted in the 1975 film *Rosebud. Time* magazine critic Richard Schickel wrote: "John Lindsay plays a U.S. Senator pretty much as he played being mayor of New York City—like a B picture leading man." The film has been called the nadir of director Otto Preminger's career.

Novelist Truman Capote had a role in the 1976 mystery spoof *Murder by Death.* Capote bragged to *People* magazine: "What Dom Perignon is to champagne, I am to acting." His performance is more analogous to flat ginger ale. John Simon, writing for *New York* magazine said, "Hitherto, I thought Zsa Zsa Gabor was unique among 'performers' in not even being able to play herself on screen; now Capote has snatched these sorry laurels from her."

Fighter Max Baer was somewhat less than riveting in movies like *The Prizefighter and the Lady, Riding High, The Iron Road,* and *The Harder They Fall.*

Babe Ruth was as wooden as his bat when he attempted to play himself in the Lou Gehrig story, *Pride of the Yankees.*

Rosie Grier rates worst performance by a football player turned actor for his role as *The Thing with Two Heads.* The highlight is when Grier punches himself in the jaw. He missed . . . and so did this film. Grier proved that two heads are not always better than one. He should have quit while he was a head.

Hollywood is the only asylum run by its inmates.
—GROVER JONES

According to Walter Slezak, television does have some advantages: "Television is a remarkable medium. You have to work five or six years in the theater, in hit shows, to make people sick and tired of you. This you can accomplish in only a few weeks of television."

On stage the comedian has to earn the audience's laughter and the material has to be funny. On television the laugh track has made good comedy writing and performing unnecessary.

Television is a kind of radio which lets people at home see what the studio audience is not laughing at.
—FRED ALLEN

Louella Parsons, gossip columnist in the heyday of Hollywood, was so used to getting her nationally syndicated column to press just seconds ahead of the deadline that she was often inaccurate as a result. She once leaked that Sigmund Freud, "one of the greatest psychoanalysts alive," was being brought to Hollywood as a technical adviser to Bette Davis's 1939 film *Dark Victory*. Freud had been dead for several months.

Boston theatrical producer John Stetson was famous for his elaborate productions with plenty of extras. During the staging of a Last Supper tableau, Stetson complained that there weren't enough actors filling the stage. When his stage manager pointed out the well-documented fact that there were only twelve guests, Stetson hollered, "I know what I want! Give me twenty-four."

Some actors have become successful directors—Richard Attenborough, Woody Allen, Paul Newman—while for others the step to director has been unsuccessful.

Antony and Cleopatra in 1971 was Charlton Heston's first directorial effort. He also starred and took a screen credit for writing—a credit he graciously shared with William Shakespeare. The film was so bad it was never released in the United States.

Cinema hero John Wayne directed and starred in *The Green Berets*. The 1968 release attempted a political statement about Vietnam. Critic Penelope Gilliatt said, "A film best handled from a distance with a pair of tongs." The movie climaxes with the now-famous scene in which the sun sets in the East.

The 1974 film *The Savage Is Loose* deals with a mother, father, and son stranded on a desert island. George C. Scott and his wife starred in this disaster about incest, which Scott also produced, directed, and distributed.

Gene Wilder, hilarious as an actor in movies like *The Producers, Young Frankenstein,* and *Blazing Saddles,* took his success too seriously and went on to bomb as a writer/director/actor in *The World's Greatest Lover*. In this case, all the world didn't love a lover. It lost at the box office.

The Last Movie (1971) nearly was for Dennis Hopper. Riding high on his success in *Easy Rider,* he directed and starred in this impossible movie about a movie crew in Peru.

Cecil B. De Mille was producing a remake of *The Buccaneer* in 1958 and hired Anthony Quinn to direct. Reviewers said it was a "slow, slack and stolid remake, practically no excitement or interest." What qualified actor Quinn to direct this swashbuckler about the War of 1812? He was De Mille's son-in-law.

The powerful studio heads oversaw movie production with a great deal of competence. As seers, however, they reached their level of incompetence, as these quotes demonstrate:

Louis B. Mayer: "Television is a plague and a curse, and I won't have any of our people working on it. And we certainly won't sell them any of our pictures."

Darryl F. Zanuck: "Video won't be able to hold on to any market it captures after the first six months. People will soon get tired of staring at a plywood box every night."

Warner Brothers publicity department decided to soften the hard-boiled gangster image of Edward G. Robinson. The publicity stunt they came up with was to photograph Robinson taking a bubble bath. The widely circulated photo backfired, though. People whispered that Robinson was a homosexual. Then the publicity department had to toughten up his image.

A disc jockey interviewing Dave Brubeck revealed his intellectual curiosity when he asked, "How many men do you have in your quartet?"

Listing from a Middletown, Connecticut, television section: "11:20 P.M.—Movie. KING'S ROW. Generally considered Ronald Reagan's best movie. He gets run over by a train. Channel 8."

One of Hollywood's great talents is the ability to take a successful movie and make a bad remake. The original *Lost Horizon,* directed by Frank Capra and starring Ronald Colman, remains a classic despite the disastrous 1973 remake. The newer version was a musical, and an unintentional disaster movie: The music was a disaster, the reviews were a disaster, and the ticket sales were a disaster. Film writer Leslie Halliwell summed it up: "An unbroken series of tedious songs." In their greed, Columbia Pictures licensed merchandise for *Lost Horizon* pillows, candles, jewelry, watches, coloring books, cookbooks, albums, planters, clothing, and perfume. Because it was one of the most expensive disasters in Columbia history, Hollywood wags dubbed it "Lost Investments."

Studio heads in the thirties and forties competed heavily to tie up the leading writers of the day. Several of America's best writers couldn't refuse the lure of movie gold. Still, with the exception of Samuel Goldwyn, the studio heads were not always in touch with the literary world. Charles MacArthur, collaborator with Ben Hecht on *The Front Page,* introduced a

London mechanic to Louis B. Mayer as the "hottest playwright in England since George Bernard Shaw." The mechanic was quickly installed in an office at MGM and was drawing a salary of $1,000 a week. Several weeks passed before Mayer caught on.

Alfred Hitchcock once reluctantly admitted to a studio executive that he didn't get to see many movies. The surprised studio executive asked, "Then where do you get your ideas?"

> What we want is a story that starts with an earthquake and works its way up to a climax.
> —SAM GOLDWYN

TIME OUT

In sports, where promotion is usually based on winning, one would expect to find only the most competent at the top. But the sports world is not just athletes. It is made up of owners, managers, teams, coaches, fans, sportscasters, and writers, all of whom provide a wide range of opportunities for incompetence. This also includes some player blunders, such as the time Roy Riegels, in the 1920 Rose Bowl game, ran sixty-eight yards the wrong way, or when Frank Thomas made two errors on one hit ball, prompting fellow Met Marv Throneberry to ask, "What are you trying to do, take my fans away from me?"

Sportswriters, commentators, fans, and players themselves have added to our wealth of memorable quotes, both by the wisdom of their remarks and by the mangling of ideas and language. In sports we find the most superstitious people on earth. Yet who could improve on both the wit and wisdom of a comment by Duffy Daugherty, who, when coach at Michigan State, said, "My only feeling about superstition is that it's unlucky to be behind at the end of the game." On the other hand, some sports reporters and television sportscasters have asked some of the worst questions imaginable.

Rod Laver won a tennis match 6–0, 6–0. In the press conference following the match, Laver was asked, ''What was the turning point?''

Track star Rick Wohlhuter was asked by a television reporter, ''Do you train differently for the 800 meters than you do for the 880 yards?'' The 800 meter race is only 200 inches shorter than the 880 yards.

Sports quotes can be both picturesque and perplexing:

Harry Balough, Madison Square Garden fight announcer, making a plea for the March of Dimes, said, ''And now the pretty little girls will press among you with their little cans. Please give till it hurts!''

Yogi Berra, baseball player, coach, and manager, said, ''If people don't want to come out to the park, nobody's going to stop 'em.''

Responding to a statement that Ernest Hemingway was a great writer, Berra asked, ''Yeah, for what paper?''

In reply to an unfavorable comment about his looks, Berra said, ''So I'm ugly. So what? I never saw anyone hit with his face.''

When asked how he liked school, Yogi said, ''Closed.''

When an admirer noticed he wore a different sweater every day and wondered if he had one in every color, Yogi replied, ''The only color I don't have is navy brown.''

When Yogi's wife said she had seen *Doctor Zhivago,* he asked, ''Oh, what's the matter with you now?''

Jerry Coleman, the former New York Yankee infielder, continued his career as a sportscaster and became famous for his faux pas.

''We're all sad to see Glen Beckert leave. Before he goes,

though, I hope he stops by so we can kiss him good-bye. He's that kind of guy.''

"Young Frank Pastore may have just pitched the biggest victory of 1979, maybe the biggest victory of the year.''

"There's a fly ball deep to center field. Winfield is going back, back. . . . He hits his head against the wall. It's rolling toward second base.''

Dizzy Dean, after recovering from a hit on the head by a thrown ball, said, "The doctors X-rayed my head and found nothing.''

Frankie Frisch, sports broadcaster, commenting on the weather: "It's a beautiful day for a night game.''

Toots Shor, restauranteur, excused himself from Sir Alexander Fleming, discoverer of pencillin, when he saw Mel Ott enter the restaurant: " 'Scuse me. Somebody important just came in.''

To Err Is Human

Old records are being broken all the time. During the 1964–1965 basketball season, Bailey Howell set an NBA record: 345 personal fouls in one season.

Major league pitcher Bobo Newsom was traded sixteen times during his career. He led the American League in losses four times.

The early Mets were considered the worst baseball team in major league history. In their first year, 1962, they won 40 games and lost 120. Some losing streaks went as long as 17 games.

Each of the following establishes a record of some kind:

On one memorable Boat Race day on the Thames, Cambridge defeated Oxford by the largest margin in history because

Oxford's shell sank. The never-say-die oarsmen continued pulling the oars until they were entirely submerged.

During a wrestling match in Providence, Rhode Island, Stanley Pinto was thrown against the ropes and got tangled up. Trying frantically to extricate himself, Pinto accidentally pinned his shoulders to the mat for three seconds. The referee declared him the loser as his opponent watched from across the ring.

A featherweight in a Golden Gloves match in Sioux Falls, South Dakota, removed his robe for the fight. He had forgotten his boxing shorts. The audience rocked with laughter as the athlete returned to the dressing room. He came back for the fight, but lost.

Minor league baseball teams from Peoria, Illinois, and Port Huron, Michigan, were locked in a tie game when Port Huron player Dan O'Leary stepped up to the plate. O'Leary hit a home run and was so excited that he ran the bases backward. The umpire ruled him out and Port Huron lost the game.

The army staged a boxing match to entertain the troops stationed in Bristol, England: Carmine Milone *vs.* Louis Fetters. When the bell rang for the first round, Milone ran from his corner, tripped, hit his head on a post, and was knocked out. Neither boxer had thrown a single punch.

In what is considered the most embarrassing play of all time, the 1926 Brooklyn Dodgers' Babe Herman hit a single with the bases loaded. The runner on third scored. The runner on second stopped at third. The runner from first took second, then slid into third. Babe Herman also slid into third, where all three players stood dumbfounded. Two of them were ruled out.

Two Brazilian soccer teams took the field for a match. The first goal was scored three seconds after the kickoff because the goalie was still on his knees praying for victory.

New York Giants third baseman Mike Grady made four errors during one play in 1895. He fielded a grounder clumsily and threw to first base. He missed. When the batter rounded second, the first baseman threw to Grady. Grady dropped the ball. Finally he recovered it and threw it home. The throw was high and the ball entered the stands.

For the 1977 Golden Gloves, Harvey Gartley battled Dennis Cullette. Gartley was counted out forty-seven seconds after the opening bell, even though he was never touched by Cullette. Gartley got so overworked he "danced himself into exhaustion and fell to the canvas."

A Turkish wrestler named Yousouf Ishmaelo always carried his fortune with him on a belt decorated with gold coins. When, on a voyage, the boat began to sink, Ishmaelo refused to discard his belt. It weighted him down and he drowned.

> I would like to deny the statement that I think basketball is a matter of life and death. I feel it is much more important than that. —LEE ROSE

9

As the World Churns

Humanity, let us say, is like people packed in an automobile which is traveling downhill without lights at a terrific speed and driven by a four-year-old child. The signposts along the way are all marked "progress".

—Lord Dunsany

The history of the world is replete with stories of species climbing out of the primordal swamp and ascending the evolutionary scale. Some find a place of complete accommodation to their environment, and others become extinct or continue the quest for further development. We may observe the clam and the earthworm, contented and at peace with their surroundings, unchanged in millions of years. We may also discover the fossil remains of the dinosaur and the dodo bird which failed to adapt to their environments and thereby became extinct. Interested though we may be in the creatures that made complete adaptation and in those that failed, we devote most of our attention to species still in the evolutionary process.

Of all the creatures struggling for competence in their interaction with the world, human beings are by far the most interesting because of their extraordinary ability to modify their environment. While other species were satisfied with a nest or burrow, we moved out of the cave to build huts, houses, apartments, skyscrapers, condominiums, and specialized facilities such as schools, hospitals, offices, and factories. We organized into towns, cities, states, and countries but never found a satisfac-

The history of the world is replete with stories of species climbing out of the primordial swamp.

tory solution, because each time we changed our environment, our environment changed our behavior, and our new behavior demanded a new environment.

Our first garments were made of animal skins. The invention of fabrics made by weaving plant fibers and animal hair was a big step, allowing for greater variety in texture, weight, and use of clothing. The new weaving process provided opportunities for the incorporation of a variety of colors and designs into the material, so the fashion industry was inevitable.

Steam-powered mills producing cotton cloth heralded the beginning of the industrial revolution, which swept the civilized world and changed the whole structure of society. The problems created by the industrial revolution, in the way we live, the way we work, and in the economic system, have not been resolved to this day.

The abundance of machine-made cloth resulted in clothing becoming more than a means of protection from the elements. Clothes for work, clothes for play, formal clothes, informal clothes, clothes for various times of day, all became part of the wardrobes of the well-dressed, providing adornment and status in almost every class of society. In the high-fashion world, competition to outdress others in order to gain social recognition resulted in the fashion designer's gaining celebrity status. Who designed the clothes became more important than what was worn, and the label of the designer was displayed on the outside of the garment.

In progressing from animal skins to natural fibers to synthetics, we have encountered many problems. The universal cleaner, soap, has been largely replaced by detergents and chemical solvents. Soap was biodegradable, but detergents with their phosphates and other chemical additives have entered our lakes, rivers, and oceans where they have stimulated algae growth, robbed the water of oxygen, and killed fish and other aquatic life. The phosphate levels in the detergents were lowered, and other difficulties in getting clothes clean presented themselves. Presoaks are now offered as a prelude to washing, additives are recommended to accompany the actual washing process, and fabric softeners are introduced in the rinsing or drying phases. As the cleaning process has become more complex, the products and equipment and environmental consequences have become more complicated. And so it goes in every area of human enterprise. Problems require solutions, and the solutions are in themselves problems that require solutions.

> PETER'S ACCUMULATION-OF-FILTH PRINCIPLE: Cleaning anything involves making something else dirty, but anything can get dirty without something else getting clean.

MEANWHILE, BACK AT THE PLANT

During the years since the merger, hiring and other personnel problems have continued to plague Akme Lead and Pewter Products, Inc. In an attempt to remedy this situation, the board,

Providing adornment and status in almost every class of society.

on the recommendation of the general manager, Jerry Attrick, appointed Conklin Mann, a recent M.B.A., as personnel manager. Copies of a series of memorandums found in one of his files indicate how this move is working out.

 AKME LEAD AND PEWTER PRODUCTS, INC.

FROM: Conklin Mann, Personnel Manager

TO: Jerry Attrick, General Manager

MEMO: J.A., glad to hear that the doctor is satisfied with your progress and that you are re-joining us here at company headquarters. The diagnosis, nervous exhaustion, is not to be taken lightly, although we are all pleased that it was nothing more serious.

Your absence makes me feel more strongly than ever that you need an assistant to take on some of your work load. You will recall that I have made this recommendation several times in the past year. I do believe the time has come when you should do something definite about it.

Kindest personal regards,
Con Mann

AKME LEAD AND PEWTER PRODUCTS, INC.

FROM: Jerry Attrick, General Manager

TO: C. Mann, Personnel Manager

MEMO: Dear Con, many thanks for your memo. I assure you, I have been giving the question of an assistant very serious consideration. I agree I should have one. In view of my recent illness, I say, NOW is the time! Trouble is that I can't see anyone in the firm who could fill the bill.

I suppose we could recruit some outsider with a sound knowledge of the lead and pewter industry, but it would be a gamble. I'd rather use someone already on the team. Any suggestions?

General Manager
J. Attrick

Akme Lead and Pewter Products, Inc.

FROM: C. Mann, Personnel Manager

TO: Jerry Attrick, General Manager

MEMO: Well J.A., I've been trying to think of someone who is right for the promotion to Assistant General Manager, but I agree with you—there's some objection to every one of them.

Stu Pidd, Molding Supervisor, after all the trouble we've had with him over the way he organizes—or fails to organize—his department. Also, he's far too friendly and easygoing with the staff.

Hy Sterik, Advertising Director. I know your opinion of him! He admits, himself, that he's in the wrong job, and is far more suited to creative work than administration.

Cal Luss, Metal Products Manager, unfortunately lives in a world of chemicals and alloys, and hardly knows what's going on in the rest of the organization.

Mal Larky, Sales Manager. Of course, he's the most ambitious of the bunch, but I hate to think what would happen if someone this aggressive and manipulative were let loose in the head office.

Ann Jyna, Office Manager. I mention her just for completeness. She's so obsessed with paperwork that she doesn't think anything else matters, and then there is her health to consider. After all, if she was a better administrator, you wouldn't be having your present problems.

J.A., it certainly is a tough problem, and at present I can't come up with an answer.

Con Mann

Akme Lead and Pewter Products, Inc.

FROM: J. Attrick, General Manager

TO: C. Mann, Personnel Manager

MEMO: Con, you're right about our department heads. You overlooked the Stores Manager and Grounds Foreman, but I'm afraid they're all the same—just haven't got what it takes.

The thought keeps crossing my mind, Con, that this ridiculous situation must exist in other firms, or how could we maintain our competitive position in the industry? There simply must be some talent in this company, if only we could bring it to light. As Personnel Manager, you are the one who should be able to tell us how.

                                   J. Attrick

Akme Lead and Pewter Products, Inc.

FROM: C. Mann, Personnel Manager

TO: J. Attrick, General Manager

MEMO: J.A., congratulations! Your analysis of the situation is right on. You know we've tested everyone in the firm, and I have the records right here. These are fine for lower-level positions, but give little help in deciding who is to take a position next to you as leader of our organization.

The Assistant General Manager should be someone who, after serving as your right-hand man, would be capable of stepping into your shoes. We are all looking forward to serving for the next three years under your dynamic leadership, but who will carry on the great traditions you have established? Your assistant must be someone whose personal characteristics are acceptable <u>to you,</u> and that's something my tests don't reveal. Here's a suggestion. I'm not trying to influence you, of course, J.A. The decision must be yours and yours alone. But it has occurred to me that we're looking at people too much in terms of their knowledge of the lead and pewter business.

Sure, J.A., you worked your way up from lead—ingot handler but the thing that accounts for your success as General Manager is essentially your ability to work with <u>people.</u> Mightn't it be better to look for a person with a broad understanding of <u>people,</u> rather than looking for technical know—how?

Con Mann
<u>PERSONNEL MANAGER</u>

Akme Lead and Pewter Products, Inc.

FROM: J. Attrick, General Manager

TO: C. Mann, Personnel Manager.

MEMO: Dear Con, I believe you've got it. I think we've both been missing the main point. I feel I need someone who really knows Personnel Practice—someone in whom I have a great deal of trust. As often happens, we miss the obvious solution, because it's right under our very noses.

It's now very clear to me that YOU, Con, are obviously best suited for the post of Assistant General Manager, and I am going to recommend this to the board. Con, I'm asking you to accept this position as my assistant.

Jerry
General Manager

AKME LEAD AND PEWTER PRODUCTS, INC.

FROM: C. Mann, Personnel Manager

TO: Jerry Attrick, General Manager

MEMO: J.A., your offer came as quite a surprise. At first I didn't think you were serious. On second thought I understood your thinking, and I can't help but agree with you.

In the interests of the future of A.L.P.P.I., it is my sincere desire to assist you in the best way I can. I accept your offer. I hope your faith in me isn't misplaced, and I promise to fulfill my responsibility, and to give YOU my best efforts in my new position.

Con

PS. J.A., I would recommend that A. Newman be promoted to the post of Personnel Manager. I hired him as my assistant because of the extra burden this department was carrying during your absence. He is a young man who shows great promise.

CM

AKME LEAD AND PEWTER PRODUCTS, INC.,

FROM: A. Newman, Personnel Manager

TO: C. Mann, Assistant General Manager

MEMO: Con, in the two years since you assumed the post of Assistant General Manager, you have shouldered an increasingly heavy load of responsibility. I was glad to hear that your medical report offers hope of your continuing as A.G.M., provided you take things easy. I know I can speak frankly, Con, and high blood pressure, along with your gastric ulcer, certainly should not be

taken lightly. Several times during the past
year, as you will recall, we've talked about
the idea of your taking an assistant to
lighten your burden a little. Con, I suggest you do this right now. It's my duty to
say this, for your health's sake as well as
for the protection of A.L.P.P.I. interests.

So, I recommend that Ann Jyna continue as
Office Manager, and that you appoint a Deputy Assistant General Manager to share the
load with you.

Your health will be protected, your peace
of mind will be restored, and there will be
greater efficiency at A.L.P.P.I. After all,
that's what we all want.

Personal Regards,
A. Newman
Personnel Manager

These memos show that even a sincere attempt to relieve incompetence may produce only further levels of incompetence.
In such circumstances, accumulation of deadwood is inevitable.
As a method of resolving problems, promotion and additional
staff always contain the possibility of counterproductivity. A
typical example of this is described in the Bible (Matthew 25:21):
"Well done, thou good and faithful servant: thou hast been faithful
over a few things, I will make thee ruler over many things."
The fact that Good and Faithful Servant has competently done
the "few things" connected with his original position does not
guarantee that he will be able to handle the "many things" that
go with the higher rank.

COROLLARY 18: The higher one climbs the hierarchal ladder,
the shakier it gets.

The criteria for evaluating competence are often quite difficult to identify. For example, James K. Polk made four ambi-

tious promises when he was campaigning for the presidency. He promised that if he was elected he would acquire California, settle the Oregon boundary dispute, lower the tariff, and establish a subtreasury. He was elected and accomplished every one of his promises. No other President even approached his record.

On July 29, 1962, a poll was conducted among seventy-five noted American historians to assess the competence of past Presidents. They rated the Presidents in five categories and placed Polk in the second group. Woodrow Wilson, who failed to fulfill his promise to keep America out of war, ranked in the top group. James K. Polk was a one-term president.

> No man will ever bring out of the Presidency the reputation which carries him into it.
> —THOMAS JEFFERSON

RUINOUS REMEDIES

Many attempted solutions to problems are unsuccessful, and there are a number of reasons why. Anne Kelly of Bristol, England, wanted to insulate her home. What actually happened was a clear case of incompetence. The workmen arrived to pump insulation into the walls. On the first try they punched a gaping hole in the living room wall. On the second, they drilled through a wall and into her deep freeze. They went outside for the third go and this time drilled through a central heating pipe and on into the kitchen. Kelly said she stood there, frozen, watching insulating foam being pumped into the kitchen. "It was like something from outer space," she said.

Other attempted solutions fail because they are the right remedies for the wrong problems or vice versa. Some are ineffective because they are false cures that were never intended to do more than fool the public.

Without attention to the interlocked outcomes, a government decision may produce a slight gain in one area and a big loss in

The criteria for evaluating competence are often quite difficult to identify.

another. Old Age Security Insurance benefits were raised to help the elderly poor, but it put them a few dollars over eligibility for Medicaid. The result was that medical coverage was denied to that population needing it most.

A government policy of strict enforcement of building codes was a well-intentioned effort to improve low-income housing. The outcome of the policy shows that owners of buildings in low-income neighborhoods will not ignore their profit-making intent because of a government policy change. Rather than face a loss, owners refused to spend large sums in order to bring their properties up to code. Instead they gave up ownership, resulting in thousands of abandoned buildings and, for many, a worsening of their housing situation.

An article in *The Washington Monthly* described our unwarranted belief in government solutions, as follows: "As a nation, we feel every problem should be solved in Washington. We cannot throw money at a problem and expect it to disappear. Democrats make that mistake with social reforms. Republicans are making it with defense programs."

> Politics is a field where the choice lies constantly be-
> tween two blunders.   —JOHN MORLEY, M.P.

Efforts to save the alligators in Florida included forbidding
owners of large swamp areas to kill the alligators. No longer
able to make a profit from raising alligators, the owners drained
the land to grow crops and the alligators were wiped out completely in the areas where they were intended to be saved.

> Every decision you make is a mistake.
> —EDWARD DAHLBERG

The congressional Office of Technology Assessment conducted a study of the results of two American embargoes aimed
at hurting the Soviet Union's economy.

When the 1979 grain embargo disrupted sales to Russia, the
Soviets found sources in other countries. The heavy losses were
suffered by U.S. farmers and the U.S. economy.

The report said that embargoes on oil and gas pipeline technology likely hurt the American economy more than the Soviets. It made the Americans appear in the world market to be an
unreliable supplier, endangering future sales and causing lingering ill will against the United States among its NATO allies who
objected to the sanctions. The report also said that the Reagan
administration's hard-line strategy produced such an outcry in
Europe that the embargo was arguably a welcome political
windfall for the U.S.S.R.

> *It can't happen here* is number one on the list of
> famous last words.   —DAVID CROSBY

One of the most effective means of escalating an activity is
to place a ban on it. The tendency to desire an object because it
is expressly forbidden produced a reverse effect for the moralistic Watch and Ward Society of Boston. The verdict ''Banned

in Boston'' was once a guarantee of huge sales for a book or a big audience for a play.

> I never knew a girl who was ruined by a bad book.
> —JIMMY WALKER

In an attempt to reduce the costs of excessive overtime for New York City police, additional officers were placed on the streets. Because the source of most police overtime is court processing of arrests, not patrol duty, the bigger patrol force meant increased arrests, more time in court, and escalated overtime.

> Time is money, especially overtime. —EVAN ESAR

Colorado instituted "sunset laws," under which regulatory agencies must be reviewed every five years and abolished unless a new law enacts their renewal. Reviews for the first year of the program cost $212,000. The results? Three part-time agencies were abolished. Their combined budgets equaled $6,810.

> If a thing is worth doing, it is worth doing badly.
> —G. K. CHESTERTON

A four-year program called the Area Redevelopment Administration passed out over $300 million in grants and long-term loans to companies operating plants in depressed areas. Because the business community condemned the program for fostering unfair competition, the ARA announced its termination as of June 30. A new program, the Economic Development Administration, was given $3 billion in funding. About 350 of the workers who were laid off from the ARA were given jobs by the EDA and were told to report for work July 1.

> The most important art of the politician is to find new names for institutions whose old names have become odious to the public.   —TALLEYRAND

A study for the Association of Life Underwriters relates that for a dollar to reach the needy, churches spend 8 cents, charitable organizations spend 27 cents, and the federal government spends $3.

> Charity creates a multitude of sins.
> —OSCAR WILDE

President Mobutu Sese Seko of Zaire spent $1 billion on a dam for the Zaire River and a 1,100 mile-long power line to the copper-producing region of Shaba. The Zaire River electricity began to flow in 1981 but eight months later was switched off permanently. Shaba is an electrically self-sufficient province.

> As worldlings do, giving thy sum of more
> To that which had too much
> —WILLIAM SHAKESPEARE

It is reassuring to know that even during a fuel shortage, vital emergency services will be in operation. During the 1973 energy crisis, 100 percent priority status was awarded to the soft-drink industry for allocation of gasoline. This was the same status enjoyed by ambulances and fire trucks. The order was made by Energy Secretary Charles Duncan, former president of Coca-Cola.

> Cheer up, the worst is yet to come.
> —PHILASTER CHASE JOHNSON

In Faversham, England, the town council voted to allocate $15,750 for a time-and-motion study to improve its efficiency. The town clerk said that officials had spent so much time with the efficiency experts that the council was six months behind in its work.

> Our business in life is not to succeed, but to continue
> to fail in good spirits. —ROBERT LOUIS STEVENSON

There was a time when the presidency was as high as one could go in an organization, but runaway inflation in job titles has devalued even that prestigious rank. Walter Shipley, chairman of Chemical Bank, is not its president. He is Chief Executive Officer and has appointed three presidents, one for each major sector. "I don't need one number-two man," Mr. Ship explained. "I need three." Three number-two men, each of whom will have the title that used to mean number one.

The proliferation of vice-presidents has made it necessary to establish a ranking order with ordinary vice-presidents at the bottom, senior vice-presidents at the next level, and only executive vice-presidents at the level that used to mean number two. In some organizations it is difficult to meet anyone who is not a vice-president or an administrative assistant (formerly secretary) to a vice-president. A company may feel that its customers will place a bigger order with a sales representative called a vice-president, thinking him or her a senior corporate executive, but it is also contributing to meaningless job titles and to deterioration of language generally.

Titles are shadows, crowns are empty things.
—DANIEL DEFOE

European agricultural experts convinced the Burmese that deep plowing would increase their crop yield. Instead it broke up the hard subsoil that held the water in the rice paddies.

The experts persuaded some farmers in Turkey to remove the stones from their land. Later it was discovered that the stony land yielded better crops, since in that dry climate, stones preserved the moisture.

An expert is one who knows more and more about less and less.   —NICHOLAS MURRAY BUTLER

The 1976 Guatemalan earthquake presented an opportunity for helpful intervention. America donated 27,000 tons of grain to help the victims. Guatemala had just harvested its largest grain crop in years. The gift knocked the bottom out of the country's grain market, creating a worse disaster than the earthquake for the people the aid was intended to help.

> The way out of trouble is never as simple as the way in.   —ED HOWE

The Aswan High Dam was intended to increase agricultural productivity by providing more irrigation water. A debilitating parasitic disease, schistosomiasis, which attacked a small percentage of the population, was a long-standing problem. The parasite is carried by snails that live in the irrigation canals. When the canals dried out each year, most of the snails died, thus curbing the disease. After the dam was built, the canals were filled year round; the snail population was uncontrolled; nearly half the entire Egyptian population suffers from schistosomiasis; the anticipated increase in productivity has been lost to the severe debilitating effect upon the workers, who lose up to half their strength; and the annual economic loss is about $550 million.

> If I had my way I'd make health catching instead of disease.   —ROBERT G. INGERSOLL

A deficit in U.S. trade with other nations occurred in 1971, the first time since 1893. Concern for the noncompetitiveness of U.S. industry was relieved when the Department of Defense presented a plan for escalating world sales of U.S. armaments from $925 million in 1970 to $3.8 billion in 1973. This was the largest single effort devised for restoring a balance of trade to the United States. Unfortunately, it was done at great risk to world stability, and the balance of trade is still in trouble.

> Who knows when some slight shock, disturbing the delicate balance between social order and thirsty aspiration, shall send the skyscrapers in our cities toppling.   —RICHARD WRIGHT

10

The Implausible Dream

> Life is a serious attempt to make something of oneself and one's surroundings, but I also see it as a marvellous thing that you're put into where you get a lot of fun out of the impossibility of it all.　　　　　—ANGUS WILSON

I have long had visions of a humane, decent, and practical society where doing the right thing was not the exception but the rule, and where the only battles were against ignorance, suffering, hunger, disease, incompetence, injustice, and war itself. While having these utopian dreams I also considered the means by which our modern declining world could change direction and move toward an ideal state. It was at this point that my utopian vision would blur and reality would come into focus.

A concept of the utopian state was created by the book *Utopia,* written by Sir Thomas More in 1516. *Utopia* described an imaginary island on which the perfection of moral, social, and political life was achieved. Two clues should have discouraged those who wanted to build the perfect society: The first was that More's title, *Utopia,* was a Latin word of Greek origin meaning "no place." The second was the improbable proposition that life on Utopia was governed entirely by reason.

> Logic is the art of going wrong with confidence.
> 　　　　　—JOSEPH WOOD KRUTCH

The utopian state is based on a belief in perfectionism. We are human, however, not because we are perfectible, but because we are variable. Although I do not believe in the perfectibility of the human species, I am convinced that individuals who make up the species are capable of improvement. As a teacher I have seen students improve in their command of subject matter, thinking skills, creativity, confidence, and ethical behavior. I have seen individuals grow and develop sufficiently to achieve self-satisfaction and to fulfill their responsibilities to themselves and to society. Unfortunately, improvability did not protect those individuals from the Peter Principle.

> How did I get here? Somebody pushed me. Somebody must have set me off in this direction and clusters of other hands must have touched themselves to the controls at various times, for I would not have picked this way for the world. —JOSEPH HELLER

I have seen competent medical practitioners promoted to become incompetent administrators of departments, clinics, and hospitals. I have seen doctors in private practice promote themselves to incompetency by becoming so interested in making money that their therapeutic role suffered. Some are neither adequate doctors nor successful financiers.

It is possible for an individual with the appropriate aptitudes to become a great physician. After achievement of competence as a medical practitioner, human variability still makes it possible for that successful individual to reach his or her level of incompetence on a higher rung of the hierachal ladder. The competent physician or surgeon with low social aptitude will find his or her rung of incompetence in personnel matters. The doctor with ethical deficiencies may find his rung of defeat through involvement in insurance fraud, illegal drugs, or kickback schemes. The brilliant therapist who has a psychological instability that causes brief lapses into carelessness could incur malpractice suits, leaving him or her without a rung to stand on. And so it goes: One successful doctor's rung of ruin will be uncontrolled drink, another's drug addiction, while a third may have injudicious sexual involvement with patients.

While a third may have injudicious sexual involvement with patients.

Fortunately, a sufficient number of doctors and other medical personnel stay at a level of competence so that most of our medical needs can be met, but each practitioner has some area of relative weakness which, through escalation, could come into play when the relevant rung is reached.

Similarly, at each level of each job or profession there is a human characteristic needed to assure competence, the absence of which spells trouble.

> If one is successful in one's craft, one is forced to leave it. The machine-tool man began in the shops; as V.P. for sales and advertising, he has become an uneasy manipulator of people and of himself. Likewise, the newspaperman who rises becomes a columnist or desk-man, the doctor becomes the head of a clinic or hospital, the professor becomes a dean, president, or foundation official, the factory superintendent becomes a holding company executive. All these men must bury their craft routines and desert their craft companions. They must work less with things and more with people.   —DAVID RIESMAN

When an individual matches his or her area of ineptitude with the competence requirements at the first rung of a particular professional ladder, we say that he or she was never cut out for the job. Another person's abilities may fit every rung to the very top of the ladder without encountering one step coinciding with his or her areas of inadequacy. Then these prodigies of success may attempt scaling another ladder—the successful sales representative starts his own business; the prosperous lawyer goes into politics; the famous reporter buys a small-town newspaper and becomes a publisher. In this way the highly successful can keep their routes to incompetence open and the truly persistent can continue ladder-hopping until they find one with their particular rung of downfall.

> My mother used to say that if you can always do a job well, then it's beneath your capabilities.
> —LINDA TSAO YANG

Some who are successful on one ladder may be tempted to straddle two or more ladders at the same time. The successful businessperson acquires a second company or a third and eventually achieves a situation completely beyond his or her control. With sufficient ingenuity and persistence, it appears that even the most talented individuals can achieve their levels of incompetence.

> I know well what I am fleeing from but not what I
> am in search of.   —MICHEL DE MONTAIGNE

With advances in technology, human error is multiplied. Power tools in the hands of an incompetent can do many times the damage possible with hand tools. A laborer digging with a spade makes a mistake and the results are inconsequential. The operator of a steam shovel makes one false move and retaining timbers collapse, foundations give way, and the building comes tumbling down.

The bookkeeper making entries in a ledger is distracted momentarily, omits one digit, and the books don't balance. A review of the columns of figures locates the error, and except for some lost time, little harm is done. The operator of a computer omits one digit and the consequences can be far-reaching, expensive, even disastrous.

> In a few minutes a computer can make a mistake so
> great that it would take many men many months to
> equal it.   —MERLE L. MEACHAM

Pharmaceuticals have become more powerful, so that greater accuracy in prescribing and taking drugs is required. Products such as pesticides used in agriculture are more toxic, requiring greater competency on the part of workers using them. Incompetence by anyone along the line in the manufacture, transportation, storage, distribution, and use of many modern chemical products can have wide-ranging, harmful results.

> Most inventions were devices for saving time, for
> shrinking space, for enhancing energy, for speeding

motions, for accelerating natural processes: devices which equipped modern man with seven league boots and magic carpets, releasing people from the physical constraints of here and now. But note the curious twist that actual experience has given to all these early plans and aspirations: the faster we travel, the less we actually see and experience on the way; the larger the area of our communication, other things remaining the same, the more limited the area of understanding; the greater our physical power, the more formidable become our social and moral limitations.

—LEWIS MUMFORD

The management and handling of nuclear arms provides the ultimate example of the need for increased competence. In the bomb dropped on Hiroshima, 12 pounds of U235 was converted into energy equivalent to the explosion of 12,500 tons of TNT. It killed more than 100,000 persons in a few seconds. Today the superpowers have the nuclear potential of billions of tons of TNT. The United States and the Soviet Union each calculate how many megatons dropped on the urban centers of the other would kill the bulk of the population. Strategists calculating the outcome of nuclear attacks base their predictions of kill power on the number of deaths by explosion and radiation fallout. They fail to predict that the bombs presently available could knock out 70 percent of the ozone layer, which, by screening lethal levels of ultraviolet rays, makes life on earth possible for Russians and Americans and everyone else. No winner would emerge from an earth devoid of human life. It would take thirty years for the ozone layer to re-form and probably millions of years for a new species to evolve and dominate the planet.

The central problem of our time—one from which our other difficulties stem—is one produced by the stagnation of the political theory during an age of technological advance. The most sophisticated machinery

is thus placed in the hands of politicians whose ideas
date from the era of the horse-drawn vehicle.
                                    —C. NORTHCOTE PARKINSON

At a time when increased competence is needed at every level
of every hierarchy, including government, education, and business, we find ourselves in a period of breakdown in moral val-
ues, deterioration of public institutions, and industrial stagnation.
Although some human error is inevitable, it is essential in this
age that it be kept at a minimum and that the operation of the
Peter Principle be controlled so that individuals are not escalated
to that rung where their incompetence will make its greatest
contribution toward the malfunction of the business, school,
government, or other organization in which they are involved.

The struggle to reach the top is itself enough to fulfill the heart of man.   —ALBERT CAMUS

My previous books of solutions, *The Peter Prescription: How
to Make Things Go Right* and *The Peter Plan: A Proposal for
Survival,* presented formulas and processes to increase personal
competence, confidence, and creativity, along with how to manage others so as to encourage and support their competence, and
how to apply these processes in solving the larger problems of
society. This present book explains the Peter Principle primarily
through actual examples and will close with a few real examples
of how individuals and organizations have tried to avoid becoming incompetent.

COROLLARY 19: Climb the ladder of success, reach the top,
and you'll find you're over the hill.

DEBUREAUCRATIZATION

A special brand of incompetence is generated by the increase in rule makers, rule enforcers, and red-tape artists com-

monly referred to as bureaucrats. Unfortunately, when a bureaucrat becomes a victim of the Peter Principle, he or she ceases to do anything useful but is still able to turn out meaningless forms and procedures that ensnare the rest of us in a tangle of paperwork, making our lives difficult. It is heartening to hear of any successful attempt to curtail this trend.

In Brazil, the bureaucracy is the ultimate in complexity. As many as 1,000 people may be in line at a government office before the doors open in the morning. If you are a manufacturer and wish to export your product, a license to do so requires 1,470 separate legal actions through 13 ministries and 50 agencies. The Brazilian government, in an effort to stem the tide of bureaucracy, has created the new Ministry of Debureaucratization. The new Minister Extraordinary of Debureaucratization, Helio Beltrão, estimates that bureaucracy costs Brazil $13 billion a year in inefficiency, as well as in delays and lost business that contribute to the nation's 120 percent inflation. So far, Beltrão has eliminated 400 million documents and has initiated only 150 directives.

Under the direction of Premier Zhao Ziyang, China has begun a reorganization of its bureaucracy. China has ninety-eight ministries, commissions, and agencies, and Zhao hopes to reduce the number to fifty-two. Twelve ministries and commissions have already been reduced to six and streamlined by reducing personnel by one third. To facilitate decision making, the Chinese intend to cut the number of ministers and vice-ministers by about three quarters and reduce overall headquarters staff by one third.

A nation stays healthy as long as it deals with its real problems, and starts to decline when it takes on peripheral issues. —ARNOLD TOYNBEE

THE MYTH OF MANAGEMENT

Management is the act of exerting influence on individuals, thereby wielding control over a business or other organization. Good management does this in such a way that a positive outcome is achieved. Bad management usually achieves a negative outcome for an organization, whether the organization be a business enterprise, school, church, social club, sports group, political unit, household, or family.

> COROLLARY 20: In a hierarchy, the potential for a competent subordinate to manage an incompetent superior is greater than for an incompetent superior to manage a competent subordinate.

A competent manager budgets, staffs, organizes, supervises, and communicates with other persons, departments, or organizations. Unfortunately, an incompetent manager can do all of these things but still fail to provide the vision required to ensure success. Companies may have managers conscientiously writing objectives, drawing administrative charts with clearly determined lines of authority, and performing all the prescribed duties, but if a domestic or foreign competitor strikes out in a new direction and comes up with an original or superior product, all that meticulous management will come to naught.

Management is not a substitute for leadership. You can't manage people into responsibility or competence, but you may be able to lead them. A competent leader may also be a good manager, but a competent manager may lack the creativity and inspirational qualities required of a real leader. A leader has the ability to see further than the rest, to set new directions, and to inspire followers to eager involvement in fresh courses of action. Many are called leaders by virtue of their being ahead of the pack or at the top of the pyramid, and that is one definition of the word *leader*. But being out front or on top denotes only position and not the other qualities of leadership. There is a significant difference between being in charge and being a leader. Leaders have leadership ability—the higher they rise, the further they see; the more they know, the more original they become, and the less likely they will be to copy what others are doing.

In 1957 a video tape recorder made in the United States cost about $50,000. It was a massive piece of equipment used primarily within the television industry. Akio Morita, head of the Japanese company Sony, saw that if this device were made much smaller and cheaper it could become a popular home entertainment item. He committed the company to the long-range goal of developing a compact, simply operated, reasonably priced home video tape recorder. In 1965, Sony marketed the world's first home-use, reel-to-reel video tape recorder. In 1975, Sony introduced the Betamax, the world's first home-use video cassette recorder.

Engineers assigned to the task worked for twenty years developing the Betamax recorder, but when it reached the market its popularity revolutionized the television industry, expanded the use of home TV sets, started the trend toward replacing home movie cameras and projectors with video cameras and players, and established a whole new industry of producing, selling, and renting video tapes for home consumption.

American television and electronics companies may be well managed, but Sony's Akio Morita provided something extra: long-range planning and leadership. There are many differences in the American and Japanese administrative styles. In Japan, management treats labor more like partners in the total enterprise. Bonuses go to the workers and they share in the annual profits. Most of the top executives of the Sony Corporation are engineers who have firsthand knowledge of research, design, and manufacturing processes. They did not reach their positions of influence by way of attendance at a school of business management.

COROLLARY 21: Colleges can't produce competence but they can produce graduates.

Recently, Americans have been studying Japanese companies, trying to find the secrets of their success. Most of their findings are lessons America had learned many years ago, before the business experts presented their theories of management and created a new social class, the administrative elite.

> All management theories become conspiracies against good management and serve mainly to cover the manager's ass.
> —T. GEORGE HARRIS, former editor of *Psychology Today,* current editor of *American Health*

In this country's pioneer days it took leadership to build the railways and then it took management to run them. Leadership has to do with vision whereas management is concerned with control. Occasionally aptitude for both resides in one individual, but frequently when a competent manager is promoted to a position of leadership we see the Peter Principle operating at its highest level.

Many managers are competent to conduct surveys, take the advice of consultants, and work with others in determining short-term objectives based on consensus. They often lack the vision to see untried possibilities.

America's pioneering companies, which led the world in invention, innovation, and productivity, are now devoted to short-term objectives and immediate profits. Market surveys determine the product line. Customers can choose only from products that already exist, so that "new improved" products are merely copies of, or minor innovations on, the same old thing.

The American automobile industry was created by inventors and designers whose cars dominated the world market. As management was promoted into leadership positions, the industry settled into a phase of bigger and bigger cars with only minor mechanical changes, along with faddish designs such as tail fins,

elaborate chrome grills, and multicolored bodies. Foreign manufacturers took the lead in producing quality—compact, com-
fortable, fuel-efficient vehicles—and American manufacturers
found themselves having to follow the trend set by progressive
foreign leadership.

> If you see in any given situation only what every-
> body else can see, you can be said to be so much a
> representative of your culture that you are a victim
> of it.   —S. I. HAYAKAWA

America's industrial decline was to be expected by any student of hierarchiology who studied the ladder to leadership.
Management students attend business schools where, through
conforming scholarship and passive consumption of business lore,
textbooks, and courses, and through conforming to university
requirements, they obtain degrees in business administration. With
experience at various management levels, and by proving to be
good and faithful followers of the policies of top management,
they qualify for promotion to positions requiring leadership. A
whole industry has grown up to meet the needs of followers promoted to leadership. Consulting firms are available to guide the
executive fearful or incapable of making decisions.

> Creative thinking may mean simply the realization that
> there's no particular virtue in doing things the way
> they always have been done.   —RUDOLPH FLESCH

Fortunately some managers with creativity and leadership
ability reach the higher executive levels and produce positive and
innovative programs.

> The great creative individual is capable of more wis-
> dom and virtue than collective man ever can be.
>   —JOHN STUART MILL

Tandem Computer of Cupertino, California, has tried to
eliminate paperwork, even avoiding written memos in favor of

personal contact. The president of the company, Jim Treybig, says, "Most companies are overmanaged. And most people need less instruction then we think."

> We can lick gravity but sometimes the paperwork is overwhelming.   —WERNER VON BRAUN

A multiproduct manufacturer, Kollmorgen Corporation, with headquarters in Stamford, Connecticut, grosses more than $200 million annually. Kollmorgen executives found that small divisions were more productive. So when any branch of the company reaches five hundred employees, it is virtually set free to operate autonomously. It then elects its own officers and board. The company's principal rule: total honesty. All employees share in the profits. The system achieves phenomenal team spirit and success. Kollmorgen's thirteen divisions are so self-sufficient that forty-five hundred employees need a corporate staff of only twenty-five. Chief executive Robert Sevigett says, "This is such an easy way to run a business, we don't understand why everybody isn't doing it."

> Success is a journey, not a destination.
> —BEN SWEETLAND

Employees of Lincoln Electric Company in Euclid, Ohio, have reason to celebrate every year when they receive year-end bonuses. In 1982, the 2,634 factory workers were paid $41,197,311 in bonuses—an average of $15,640 per employee. Since 1934 the company has paid more in bonuses than in regular wages. Though its sales declined 25 percent in 1982, the company did not lay off any employee who had been with the company more than two years—their policy since the thirties. All work is done on a piecework basis. The harder one works, the higher the bonus. The company has never had mandatory retirement. The high worker-productivity results in lower labor costs which are passed on to the consumer. Lincoln is a world leader in the manufacture of arc-welding equipment. The company vice-president of sales says: "We feel every job in our company is an important job. We treat all our employees with dignity and respect. Our workers want responsibility. They want recognition. . . . We treat our employees as people rather than as a commodity."

> The moral point is that everything is extremely complex and difficult and it mustn't be supposed that any of it can be done by rubbing a button and saying "Abracadabra." . . . life can be more satisfactory if people don't think there are easy answers.
>   —ANGUS WILSON

Most large companies that depend to a great extent on their research have developed some means of rewarding creative, scientific, and technical personnel without promoting them out of their area of competence. In this way they avoid the risk of losing an able technical employee of real value while gaining a manager of perhaps lesser value, or in the extreme case, losing a creative scientist and gaining an incompetent administrator.

> COROLLARY 22: Being frustrated in your work can be disagreeable, but the real disaster may be when you're promoted out of it.

The way the system works was explained in an article by Gerald Meyer in the *St. Louis Post-Dispatch,* "How Monsanto Copes With Peter Principle." The Monsanto Company can promote a scientist or engineer in two ways: first, into management positions with higher administrative responsibilities, and second, into higher levels of research with greater individual responsibility.

Meyer writes:

> The second ladder is in some ways similar to promotion in the academic community. The similarity is indicated by

198 WHY THINGS GO WRONG

the names given to rungs on the Monsanto program's advancement scale. Persons selected for promotion in the program are called by stages, "Fellows," "Senior Fellows," and "Distinguished Fellows." Such titles are more suggestive of a university than of a corporation.

A typical example of a person selected for promotion is Kuen Young Kim, who was forty-two when he became a Fellow. A native of Korea, Kim received a doctorate in chemical engineering at the University of Wisconsin. He had worked at Monsanto for eleven years at the time of his promotion. He had written a number of scientific papers, had made important contributions to Monsanto's inorganic chemical division, and had worked for five years primarily in research on polishing agents used in toothpaste and other dentifrices. Monsanto is the largest manufacturer of these polishing agents.

The program is designed to reward those who have contributed significantly over a sustained period, rather than those who have achieved one or two specific successes. When a Fellow is finally chosen, his or her position within the corporation changes. The promotion is regarded as fully equivalent to advancement into a management job, and it involves corresponding salary increases. As a science Fellow, Kim will also be given greater control over the direction of his work and will not be limited by a job description.

It is believed that the success of Monsanto's program is due in large part to the careful review used in the selection process so that the title *Fellow* is taken seriously.

> The best executive is the one who has sense enough
> to pick good men to do what he wants done, and self-
> restraint enough to keep from meddling with them
> while they do it. —THEODORE ROOSEVELT

An article in the management section of the September 28, 1974, *Business Week* described the structure and operation of

Heublein, Inc. A producer of distilled spirits, Heublein had recently become a multinational company with products as diverse as Kentucky Fried Chicken, Smirnoff vodka, and Italian Swiss Colony wine. The corporation gives those in charge of each product line almost as much power and responsibility as if they were independent companies. A goal is to make the top executives, middle managers, and supervisors of each component company acutely aware of their contributions to earnings per share.

The article contained a description of the method Heublein hoped would avoid the problems created by the Peter Principle. It is called the fallback position and consists of assuring a "promoted executive, before he ever leaves his old job, that he can come back to a position of at least equal status and compensation if he does not work out."

Hicks Waldron, Heublein's president, explained:

> The corporation must accept some of the risks involved in moving this fellow up the ladder. If he gives it hell but falls short of performing satisfactorily, then I think this company has an obligation to move him back to the level he came from. He has proven that he is successful there.

The fallback position was not a new concept, but formalizing it as company policy was unusual. As Richard C. Farr, vice-president for human resources, said, "What we have done is make it an integral part of our total management planning program." One advantage is that it eliminates an employee's fear of being fired from a job he or she cannot handle.

COROLLARY 23: More competent individuals resign than incompetents get fired.

KNOW THYSELF

Most people struggle to achieve a rung on the ladder of success where they hope they will be happy, respected, and affluent. My interviews with individuals of low, middle, and high stations in life have convinced me that everyone wants success, but they define success in two ways. Success is described first as accomplishment—the acquisition of money, power, status, and possessions. Second, success is seen as achievement of happiness—a satisfying life-style, love, health, self-actualization, leisure to enjoy the beauty of this wonderful world, and time for play.

It appeared that the truly successful person was one who combined these two aspects of success in ways that gave that individual both the joy of accomplishment and the satisfaction of self-fulfillment. Those who thought that success was achieved only through climbing the accomplishment ladder were often disappointed and unhappy. Those climbers whose gaze was always focused on the rung above failed to appreciate the view from the rung they were on. Their feelings of satisfaction on attaining a new level were short-lived because they were soon striving for another level.

> COROLLARY 24: The ability of the potentially competent erodes with time, while the potentially incompetent rises to a level where his or her full potential is actualized.

Those who climbed to a level where they found opportunities for self-fulfillment, and remained at that level for a lengthy stay, and then moved forward, improving their on-the-job performance while they developed a satisfying life-style, were the most completely successful individuals I encountered.

> Why should we be in such a desperate haste to succeed, and in such desperate enterprises? If a man does

Success is seen as achievement of happiness.

not keep pace with his companions, perhaps it is because he hears a different drummer.
—HENRY DAVID THOREAU

The ingenuity shown by individuals attempting to remain
where they are msot competent is impressive in its variety. Duane
Ford, a teacher and coach at Central Columbia High School in
Bloomsburg, Pennsylvania, is an inspiring example. Ten years
ago, when I first became acquainted with him, I was impressed
with his daily teaching schedule, which included such courses
as philosophy, psychology, sociology, anthropology, econom-
ics, and political science, along with coaching the basketball team.

In only a few short years in the classroom he had earned respect and esteem as a teacher. The courses he taught were all
electives and had titles that would scare most young people, yet
all his classes were solidly booked. He was surely a perfect can-
didate to move onward and upward, but he told me he would

resist the suggestions, encouragements, bona fide offers, and enticements to "go into administration," "move up to college teaching," "leave education and come work for us and double your salary in a year."

Over the decade, aside from accepting the chairmanship of the Social Studies Department—which allowed him to retain all of his previous teaching and coaching duties—Duane has remained an inspiration to others striving to maintain and enhance their lives at their individual levels of competence.

In an interview for this book, he confessed that his strategy for staying in the job he liked was quite simple. In the peripheral areas of his work he had strived to exhibit just enough apparent incompetence to cast serious doubt on his fitness for other responsibilities. He said, "You're only as competent as your last major effort, but even a little well-placed irrelevant incompetence is like that 'ring around the collar' commercial. It may only appear now and then, and is usually quite harmless. But everyone remembers it."

Early in his career, when white shirts, solid ties, and gabardine or flannel suits were in fashion, his wardrobe consisted of brightly colored shirts, paisley ties, and madras jackets, most of which drew raised eyebrows from superiors. However with today's "anything goes" attire, he lamented, "This technique is no longer effective. It is only the students that notice my garb is out of step with both the past and present." He is seriously considering returning to the formal style of the past to create the impression that, if promoted, he would be an out-of-date administrator.

His desk calendar seldom shows the right date, and while punctual for class, he seldom arrives on time for "busy work" duties. He stresses that lateness must be alternated with occasional punctuality, or even early arrival, as: "Always being five minutes late shows some sense of organization."

There is no doubt that Duane has a well-developed sense of humor and that he enjoys the role of competent teacher unworthy of promotion. He has achieved that delicate balance, taking his teaching responsibilities seriously but not taking himself too seriously. In his teaching he uses humor to achieve classroom atmosphere, to direct attention to the relevant points in the lesson, and to resolve difficulties that may arise.

The outstanding success of his teams has always made it difficult to question his skill, dedication, and enthusiasm in the athletic arena, but even as a coach he has been able to create at least some lingering doubt. While the school's colors were blue and white, his teams appeared for three years in red-and-white uniforms with a little blue trim for the sake of tradition.

When he first came to Bloomsburg, he made a point of demonstrating an ignorance of the sports in which he was not involved. Arriving late at the first home wrestling match, he apologized at the door for "missing the first quarter." After securing a seat, he pointed to the mat in the center of the floor and blurted out in mock amazement, "Where are the ropes?"

The field hockey players new to his class were confused but charitable when he inquired, "How does the puck slide on grass?"

The cross-country race enthusiasts responded to his loud cheering at the announcement of his school's high scores in the same way a golfer would to congratulations for shooting in the high nineties. When he was corrected he dismissed the criticism with the comment "Any sport in which the low score wins deserves to be misunderstood."

Some adults fail to understand his willingness to be the butt of his own jokes, while his students see it and appreciate it as just another aspect of his sense of humor. In answer to those who may consider some of his misbehavior immature, he noted at a recent banquet honoring one of his championship teams: "I don't know what I want to do when I grow up, or even if I want to grow up, but it probably won't be much different from what I'm doing now."

In summary, I see Duane Ford as an individual who has risen to his level of competence as an outstanding teacher, coach, and wit, and who is now moving forward, improving the quality of his life and work while enjoying a sense of accomplishment and personal fulfillment.

> There is nothing more common than to hear of men losing their energy on being raised to a higher position, to which they do not feel themselves equal.
>
> —KARL VON CLAUSEWITZ

LAUGHTER—THE BEST MEDICINE

In writing about the Peter Principle it was never my intention to decry the sins, mistakes, vanities, and incompetence of my fellow human beings. I am at least as guilty as they. I have set forth my observations because I wanted to share the relief I find in laughter—that most satisfying coping mechanism whereby our personal misadventures and the general human condition are seen to be absurd.

> My way of joking is to tell the truth. It's the funniest joke in the world. —GEORGE BERNARD SHAW

A man climbing to his level of incompetence seems to be inherently more worthy of attention than a man slipping on a banana peel. The man unaware of the banana peel who slips and falls is not as amusing as a man slipping on his own pomposity. The man who sees the banana peel, confidently steps over it, and then disappears down a manhole is much funnier to me.

> If loves makes the world go round, surely humor must keep it on its axis. —EDWIN B. GILROY

Some examples of incompetence are at least as funny as any contrived comedy situations. Shirley Allard was on her first day of work as a school-bus driver in Geenfield, Massachusetts. With

two students on board, she got lost on the freeway and kept
driving till she ran out of gas—eight hours later and seventy miles
from her destination. The bus was towed to a gas station, but
since Mrs. Allard didn't have the $32 for gas and towing, she
and her weary passengers were taken to the police station. The
parents of the two boys, aged ten and eleven, had filed kidnap-
ping reports. Mrs. Allard resigned on the spot. The Salvation
Army put her up for the night and paid her bus fare home.

> Laugh at yourself first, before anyone else can.
> —ELSA MAXWELL

Incompetence can have serious consequences, but if we
eliminated all foibles and time-wasting from our lives we could
become so efficient that we would have no fun at all. When we
are children we laugh at many things but as we mature we realize the importance of an education, we have career goals, and
we struggle with the serious business of living. These activities
tend to cloud our vision so that we fail to perceive the irony in
the serious struggle to attain a level of perpetual unhappiness.

> A sense of humor keen enough to show a man his
> own absurdities as well as those of other people will
> keep a man from commission of all sins, or nearly,
> all, save those that are worth committing.
> —SAMUEL BUTLER

Stephen Pile of London, England, built his reputation as a
writer through seeing the humor in his own and others' incompetence. It is Stephen's thesis that success is overrated and that,
although everyone craves success, our talent lies not in our capability but in our incompetence. He believes that incompetence
is the quality that marks us off from lower animals and we should
learn to revere it.

He admits that occasionally a competent like R. Buckmin-
ster Fuller creates a geodesic dome which is stronger and lighter

Our talent lies not in our capability but in our incompetence.

than any previous building, but most of us go on nailing two-by-fours together in the same old way, occasionally hitting our thumbs with hammers. Those exceptional individuals who rise above the fumbling herd serve to show how badly the rest of us are doing.

As president of the Not-Terribly-Good Club of Great Britain, Stephen attempted to organize an International Festival of Incompetence at Royal Festival Hall in London. It was to be the first presentation of the world's worst singers, magicians, actors, athletes, and other performers in one grand celebration of human ineptitude. The arrangements got fouled up and administrative difficulties arose so that the festival failed to materialize.

The crowning low point in Stephen's unsuccessful presidency of the Not-Terribly-Good Club was his writing of an official handbook for the organization, *The Incomplete Book of Failures.* Unfortunately, the book was a great success. He was no longer a failure and so was expelled from the club. Even as a failure, he had failed.

> There should be a Nobel Prize for wit. Physicists, chemists, economists we can, in a pinch, do without. Peace we generally do without. Wit is indispensable.   —GEORGE F. WILL

It has never been my intention, even when writing about solutions, to do others' thinking for them. In quest for competence I was only trying to solve my own problems. In writing about it, my highest ambition was to achieve what William K. Zinsser described when he said, "What I want is to make people laugh so that they'll see things seriously."

> It is much easier to do and die than it is to reason why.   —G. A. STUDDERT-KENNEDY